Void 2 Value

Where is God in the mess of life?

Compiled by Rowena Hicks

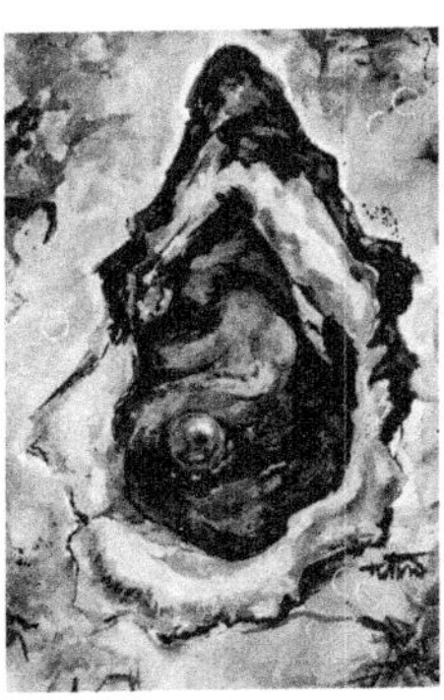

Also quoted:
Mumford & Sons. (2012). Babel. [CD]. Gentlemen of the Road/ Glassnote Records.

Helser, J. D., & Helser, M. (2018). I Am Your Beloved. [Song]. Beautiful Surrender. Bethel Music.

PLATYPUS
PUBLISHING

Contents

Introduction

Rowena Hicks

This book is for everyday people, written by everyday people who recognise that we are all imperfect and yet God comes to meet us when life gets messy.

Void 2 Value was birthed one sunny afternoon in Cambridge, England, when Elaine and I sat in her garden discussing our situations and the challenges we faced, asking why we were still waiting for the answers to prayer that we had for so long been asking for. Where was our miracle? We'd been at a conference where speakers were describing amazing miracles of all kinds, but we were still apparently waiting for ours.

We prayed, chatted some more, and came to the conclusion that we may not have had one massive miracle, but God hadn't left us alone for one moment, and we could see His intervention, comfort and support so many times over the years. Perhaps that was our miracle? It was then we decided to start to share our stories of where God had turned up in the messy lives we seemed to live; and so the podcast was launched. And now the book, to allow others to also share their stories that had so impacted both of us.

And they have defeated him [Satan] by the blood of the Lamb and by their testimony. Revelation 12:11 (NLT)

I've struggled to know and understand my true value and my identity during many periods of my life. This hasn't meant I haven't loved God and served Him. What it has meant, is that I hadn't realised my potential, to live as a new creation, letting go of my past mistakes and walking into the fullness of who He calls me to be, and what He calls me to do. As you read the stories of those who have been able to step into this new arena (and they are varied!), I hope it may inspire you to do the same.

> Instead of your shame you will receive a double portion, and instead of disgrace you will rejoice in your inheritance. Isaiah 61:7 (NIV)

Have you ever stopped to consider the words you use to describe yourself?

Today, as you read this book, if you feel in any way as if you are second best, not enough or a failure, God says 'You are His treasure.' Just as in Matthew 26:7 when the woman anointed Jesus' body in an extravagant demonstration of worship, He says to you today 'He sees your prayers and your worship. He hears what you say in the secret place, and He loves those quiet times with you. He values them highly. He values YOU highly.'

Don't underestimate the power of God's love for you or His pleasure when you share your heart. I previously attached my identity to times of failure, mistakes and loss. Today, I hope as you read these stories, you will join me in agreeing to take off that old identity and move forward in the true identity Christ has offered each of us as His beloved children, sons and daughters of the King. He has forgiven us and freed us.

I pray that as you read through the book, you will be encouraged, maybe sometimes challenged, but mostly that you come to fully understand Jesus loves you more than any of us can fully understand.

Search for the Void 2 Value podcast on major platforms.

1

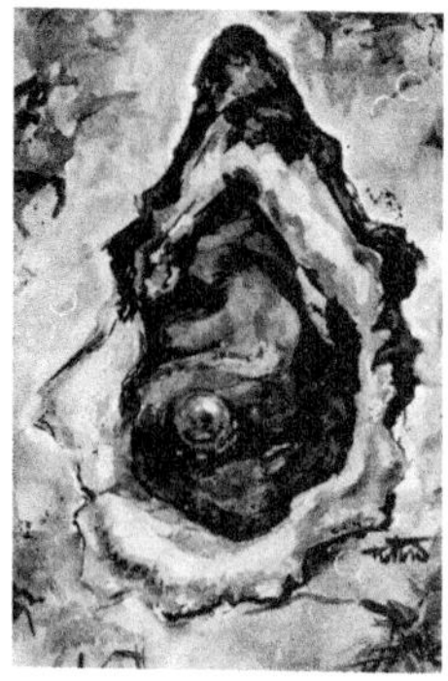

Oysters are a safe haven

Rachel's story

To me oysters are a safe haven. This came to me when I was an art student in 2024. The shape of the oyster shell became a safe, enclosing space that one could crawl into, away from harm. Although this project stemmed from dissociation and how within that dissociative state I am like a child looking for a safe place, the concept grew and evolved and I believe God has been revealing to me, even to this day, what this project means.

Water has always been a fascination; I researched a lot into sensory deprivation tanks and even the womb and the amniotic fluid that surrounds a foetus. When I read more biblical stories I saw how God works with water. The miracles Jesus performed: walking on water, water into wine and the calming of the storm. God is able to calm the storm I was in, giving me a safe place to stay and 'recharge', but He kept me safe there in my oyster shell.

I grew up in church and knew of God from a very young age, but my church left me feeling alone more often than not and I stopped attending. I still had faith and often prayed to God, especially when I was scared, which was often, unfortunately. I was in and out of the doctors' from the age of thirteen, with various tests due to an unknown gastrointestinal infection and these experiences left me with major anxiety issues and depressive episodes causing me to struggle to even attend school, let alone get an education.

But with time and therapy, I regained my confidence and I am now in a place I would never have imagined, doing things so beyond my younger self's expectations. I am currently in my second year of university and doing great. I use my experiences and lack of memory from a troublesome childhood to fuel my work, using art as a sort of personal therapy. I have started attending church again and love the family God has provided me with. The support there has kept me alive, and I am forever grateful. I was recently baptised and I was able to share my testimony with my church. Whatever battles I am facing, whether physically, mentally or spiritually, they are always there to support and love me.

Void 2 Value came to me through some interesting connections and when I found out the logo was an oyster with a pearl, I knew God was involved within the creation and connection. As mentioned before, oysters are a safe haven for me but not only that, they are also a symbol of hope that even though I may have to retreat into the shell at times, I will always emerge, seeing that small glimmer of light from the surface, a sparkle of hope.

When told about the idea of how God creates beauty from pain it mirrored for me the way an oyster turns a small bit of grit into a beautiful pearl. It shows how hope is always there even when things seem dim – hope is always there. The word HOPE breaks down into Hold On, Pain Ends.

God often works through pain, but it is all part of His greater plan. God has worked through my pain, and I can honestly say I am grateful for each tear I have shed as they are 'seeds that will reap songs of joy'.

> Those who sow with tears will reap with songs of joy.
> Those who go out weeping, carrying seed to sow, will return with songs of joy, carrying sheaves with them.
> Psalm 126:5–6 (NIV)

I am only twenty and life hasn't been an easy ride, but everything I have fought through has made me into the person I am today, someone I am proud of, even if I struggle to believe it. God is working in my life every day and I pray that He will continue, sculpting me into the daughter that does His work beautifully. I am who I am because of my faith and love for Jesus, and I wouldn't change that for anything. No words or actions against me will break this relationship between a Father and His daughter.

2

Free to be me

Ang's story

For fifty odd years I've run around with a superhero's cape around my neck. Running because my superpower was unfortunately not flying! I had to fix every problem that was presented to me, even trying to fix things that were not mine to fix.

Superpower mode always seemed to be on alert in supermarkets. Trying to help vulnerable old dears who really needed me to reach to the top shelf for them. Actually, they were quite capable of reaching themselves, thank you very much! I just needed to help them.

I was a good carrier of people's pain. I would walk into a crowded room and hoover up everyone's emotion, then leave and arrive home wondering why I felt so flat. Empathy is a beautiful gift but it can also be a burden. Compassion fatigue is a real thing.

I grew up in a Jesus-loving family. The teaching from our church and youth group was Jesus first, Others next, Yourself last. I followed that literally, without realising it was slowing killing my soul. It was distorting my relationship with my creator.

I thought that's what He wanted. I was doing all this helping, carrying, listening, empathising and fixing. All for Him. I knew in my mind that Jesus loved me and died for me. I didn't have to earn his forgiveness but subconsciously, I believed serving Him meant He would love me more.

It came as a surprise to me, but not to those who were closest to me, when I became gradually burnt out. Describing burnout is not easy. I felt washed out, had brain fog and I wanted to hide from everyone. I was told that I needed to take as much time off as I needed.

Most days I sat watching TV, or walked by the sea desperately hoping that I wouldn't bump into anyone I knew! I felt like I had no energy for anything. I napped daily. Resting did not come easy to me. I was brought up to do, do, do. I believed, wrongly, that God loved me more when I was serving Him. So, what would my relationship with God look like if I did nothing for Him?

I couldn't go to home group or prayer meetings. I couldn't cope with people talking or debating. The guilt was heavy, feeling that I was letting people and God down. My loved ones kept speaking truth to me, telling me that I was loved by them and by God unconditionally.

When anyone would talk to me describing anything in detail, my brain would feel like cotton wool and I could no longer compute what they were saying. My response would be, 'You're using too many words.'

At the beginning of 2024 I had started to read the Bible through in a year. Why? I thought it's a good Christian thing to do! I was six months in, literally reading chunks of Scripture each day. And I guess feeling pious about it. During my not-doing-anything period, I still wanted to tick off my readings for the day so I struggled on.

One night I couldn't sleep and I felt God say to me, 'I want you to stop the Bible plan.' I screamed in my mind, 'I'm six months in, what a waste! What am I supposed to do then?' He said 'Read Psalm 46:9 every day.' *'Be still and know that I am God.'* Such a well-known verse, one that I knew. I immediately deleted the Bible reading plan from my phone and it was as though I had been given a spiritual pass!

All my life I have been told to read the Bible and pray. I remember one time as a young child coming downstairs in a mood. My mum said to me 'Have you had your quiet time?' Thinking that if I had, I wouldn't or shouldn't be in a mood. I can't remember what my reply was!

I read that verse daily in different versions until it sunk in. Mostly I got the word over and over, just *'be'*. I didn't know how to do that. I felt I had to go back to basics with God and relearn what it meant to be a follower of Jesus, a child of God.

I want to say that I have learnt the following words but I know that this is something I will have to keep learning: 'I do not have to earn his love or forgiveness or acceptance. I have to just let Him love me.'

I gradually started to heal and re-entered life. It was still scary going out. I worried what to tell people. I didn't pick up on the doing again. I became more conscious of the word 'should' and started to stay clear of doing things that I thought I should be doing.

I journalled my journey that eventually turned into a blog. I have never had so many people respond as they did to that blog. So many have been or are going through some kind of suffering and as Christians we hide behind our good Christian mask. With every question of 'How are you?' we so easily lie and say 'I'm fine'.

I'm not saying we have to blurt out our true state of being to everyone. We need a trusted inner circle of people that we can share that with. I am a vicar's wife, so it's a very public life. So being vulnerable and honest was hard but I think when we are, we are giving people a gift so that they too can be vulnerable back.

Being real is freeing. Jesus came to set us free – free from bondage, free from condemnation, free to be the person He has called us to be. As I stood down from helping run things at church it then gave others the boldness to do the same. False guilt is a real thing but something that needs to be eradicated from our churches. Volunteers are getting worn out from doing. I think we need to keep short accounts with Jesus and ask him what he wants us to be doing, not what we think he wants us to do.

My quote has always been, 'Don't be a Martha, she made sandwiches that Jesus never ordered.' Martha gets a bashing about serving when Jesus wanted her to be like Mary and be at his feet listening. I don't believe Jesus is saying 'Do is bad'; I think he wants us to know when and what we should be doing. And then get the balance between resting and serving.

Jump forward to Maundy Thursday 2025. I was sitting in a stunning old church. The altar was so far away you needed binoculars to see what was happening! The beautiful Bishop Eleanor started her sermon. In the middle of her talk, she said these words, 'Jesus says "Let me love you".'

Woah, that so got my attention. I realised afresh that I was still not grasping this. I said to Jesus 'How do I let you love me?' He quietly replied, 'Let me in, let me love the parts that you try and hide from me.' That's now my restarting point. I'm going to keep letting Him in, keep letting Him love me and see where that leads me.

These are the verses that I am going marinate into my soul:

Who then is the one who condemns? No-one.
Christ Jesus who died – more than that, who was raised to life – is at the right hand of God and is also interceding for us.
For I am convinced that neither death nor life, neither angels nor demons, neither the present nor the future, nor any powers, neither height nor depth, nor anything else in all creation, will be able to separate us from the love of God that is in Christ Jesus our Lord.
Romans 8:38–39 (NIV)

It's pretty mind-blowing that absolutely nothing can separate me from the love of God. In my mind I think I'm testing Him with a list. Would He still love me if I don't go to Bible study ever again?; if I start swearing? (I was never allowed as a child); if I don't listen to sermons online again; what if I skip my Bible reading for the day? And with each testing question His loving reply was 'I would still love you.'

Just recently I went to visit a friend's farm. I love lambs and she had a few coloured Ryland sheep. The lambs looked more like chubby toddlers than newborns. I cheekily asked if I could hold one. The farmer's wife said, 'You can if I can catch one.'

After a few minutes she had caught one and she handed me a chunky lamb. It squirmed in my arms for a little bit; I am sure she was wondering what the heck was happening. I talked quietly to her and told her how gorgeous she was as I cuddled the lamb to my chest. She moved her head away from me then suddenly snuggled into my neck. We had a moment of connection; I felt she was cuddling me back.

I thought later of Jesus the good shepherd, how He holds us. Even when we are struggling against Him not appreciating His love for us and all He wants us to do is rest in His love and cuddle Him back.

I love the song 'I am your beloved' by Jonathan David Helser and Melissa Helser.

I am your beloved, you have bought me with your blood
And on your hand, you've written out my name.
I am your beloved, one the Father's love
Mercy has defeated all my shame

Further on it says:

Oh the one who knows me best
Is the one who loves me most
There is nothing I have done
That could change the Father's love.

I listen to this song regularly to let it seep in. To help me to grasp it's never about me or what I can do for Jesus. It's all about Him and letting Him love me and live through me. I would like my life to look like me walking in the love of God and only letting His love seep through me so that if and when I serve, I will be serving from a place of love not out of duty.

3

When the body stops cashing cheques!

David's story

So this is a story rather similar to one of those old cartoons, where a character realises they're carrying something far too heavy and, because they've now realised it, they promptly get flattened by it. Seventeen-and-a-half years into running a small IT business, at the end of 2021 I found myself abruptly unable to cope with even minor stressors...

The run-up to the events in question is shaped by COVID. Working in IT support, the impact on our part of the world had been considerable: when lockdowns hit, everyone needed laptops and a cloud migration, both of which felt less available than toilet paper was at the time. Demand for our services went through the roof, our workloads were out of control and we often had to spend cash to secure stock of laptops.

Unfortunately, many organisations were deeply uncertain about their ability to cover staff salaries and so felt unable to pay invoices – we sadly saw a number of clients go under in those first two years. Quite early on, a key member of our team nearly died from COVID and throughout this period some got ill, some lost close family members, one of the team had a baby that they weren't allowed to see because of the hospital restrictions – it was an HR tsunami which we had to try to take in our stride.

Whilst I was on interminable back-to-back video calls, we had two kids needing homeschooling. I must confess I had almost no involvement in that beyond being conscripted into Joe Wicks PE sessions, something we maintained as a family far longer than most sane people did. Doing what I could to support our children on their respective journeys was both a joy and a blessing for the limited windows I had: it was a wonderful time to get close to our children and invest in them in ways that would otherwise likely not have happened.

With the plague both on our doorstep and running amok in the business, and with days that were saturated with activity from start to finish, my wife started to get unwell. Without going into too much detail, after months of misleading investigations, it turned out she had breast cancer. Following her surgery, almost immediately after receiving the news that the intervention had been a success, came the news that the scan they'd done to check the results had picked up something else, and could she please come back in for a scan on her brain, which revealed a tumour on her pituitary gland.

Suffice to say the ride, like for many others, was not a smooth one. Approaching the end of 2021, two events stand out. The first was shortly after meeting with a potential new client. I had been to see the leaders of a charity to present our company offer to them and I felt the meeting had gone really well. I was on my way back to the office and was changing from an overground train to the tube at Waterloo, when I was suddenly overcome by dizziness and almost collapsed in the middle of the station. Making my way slowly to a bench, I sat in a daze for about an hour unable to stand or go and buy myself some water. It was a shocking experience and for the first time in my life I felt truly fragile. I had to call my colleagues and explain I wasn't going to be able to make it back and I needed to try and get home.

The other event was when my son invited me to come and watch an international football match on TV with him. I have no particular interest in football and the two nations playing were relatively obscure so I had no vested interest in the game, yet within no time at all and for reasons beyond my understanding at that point, the stress of the match impacted me so much I felt I was going to throw up and I had to leave the room.

These were very strong signals to me that things were not right and I was going to need to figure out what was going on. As we were in December at that point, I was fortunate enough to be able to plan a three-week holiday over the Christmas period (it's often a quiet time in the IT world) and try and figure out what to do.

My first port of call was to contact a counsellor that I had already worked with. I'd spent about a year working with her five years previously, so it was quite straightforward to book in to see her again. It felt like she was extremely quick to spot what was going on: I vividly recall her saying this was almost a textbook example of a midlife crisis. She went on to say, 'it's like watching one season dying in you, and a new one struggling to begin.'

She recommended a couple of books: one with quite an unhelpful title, Dr Tim Cantopher's *Depressive Illness, the Curse of the Strong* (which is *much* better than it sounds), and Tony Horsfall's *Spiritual Growth in a Time of Change: Following God in Midlife*. Starting with the former, quite early on Cantopher sets out a description of the person prone to this type of burnout which I felt rather accurately described me. It was encouraging to think I therefore might find targeted help in those pages, which included a clear explanation of the way antidepressants work, and why they might serve in the situation I found myself. That was all the encouragement I needed to book a phone appointment with my GP whilst on holiday with the in-laws, to whom I announced I was off to the pharmacy to go get some exciting new pills.

The second book was equally useful, albeit in very different ways. In it Horsfall describes the different phases of midlife and what the features of that journey look like, as they have been observed and documented over the years by people in different spiritual traditions. Again, it was comforting to find that I was definitely not alone in finding a crisis at this stage in my life and it was comforting to think that this was potentially another map out of the mess.

He was also particularly strong on the theme of seasons, a term that was starting to chip away at an assumption I was holding: that a calling was necessarily for life. Fluid IT was a social-purpose business that had always had a powerful sense of calling for me, without which it never would have lasted as long as it had, but that was all starting to shift.

One of the recommendations common to both books was to go away on retreat. So not long after our three-week holiday, I found myself trying to explain to my wife and team that I was going to need another week off.

I made my way up to the north of the UK where I stayed for

a few days with some friends who run a retreat centre in the Yorkshire Dales. One of the key messages I had taken from the books was that if I tried to continue as-is, things were going to get worse not better. Fundamentally, something had to change, otherwise I'd be in a downward spiral of fall apart, rest, start again, fall apart worse, etc.

The problem was, with a calling to run an IT company, how do you do that differently? I couldn't see that a day off each week would make much difference – things always bleed across that kind of boundary. I didn't think I could tell clients 'I'm not working in this business two days a week.' When you need to respond to cyber incidents, an out-of-office 40 per cent of the time is not going to go down well with clients. So, I wondered about spreading two days off across the week, working 4.8 hours a day instead of 8 hours... but I figured that would mean work would overspill all the time and it would be impossible to defend in practical terms. I was stuck.

This was all unlocked for me when a friend took me out for a walk on the Dales. It was a windy day so conversing meant we were shouting at each other as we climbed, and as I explained this conundrum to him, he thought about it and asked; 'Well, if you don't think you can quit your job, and you can't see that part-time would work, what would give life?' I remember thinking 'Oh! I know *that* question! I can answer *that*!'

Right at the end of 2017 I had started working with an Ignatian Spiritual Director, who had taken me through a process called the Exercises. Part of that involves doing a review of each day:

What am I grateful for?
What have I learned?
What brought life?
What dragged me down?
Where have I messed up and what needs forgiveness?
What am I hoping for?

At the end of each week, you look back over each of your daily reviews, and rewrite the highlights. And then once a month, you go back over the weekly reviews, and again, rewrite the highlights of the highlights. Each of these serves as a distillation and it is a process that has been absolutely transformative for me – I love it!

I'm enormously grateful that this process starts with exploring and cataloguing gratitude each day. Even at its driest, this process felt like the scaffolding that kept me going through the worst of all the pressured times: it turns out that even in the messiest parts of that, there was so much to be thankful for.

So, when my friend asked his question, it was one I was intimately familiar with and it felt easy to go digging around internally for the answers. And for the first time in a period of immense confusion, some clarity emerged: 'I want an overlapping day off with my wife' was an answer that surfaced almost immediately, and there was more to come. I wanted to be in the office with my colleagues a bit more; I wanted to make sure I made it to the Wednesday lunchtime service at a church in the City I've now been attending for 20 years. And with a little petulance, 'I want to swim in London again: I get better headspace in a 50-metre pool than in the local one which is shorter and more crowded!'

What emerged was a recipe where my week included a day off with my wife, and then two half days (neither of which needed an out-of-office.) That was what it took to get to a pattern I could at least survive and maintain whilst I tried to figure out what bigger changes might look like.

I continue to use that question 'what brings life?' to help figure that out. As I went on exploring midlife and the theme of seasons, it felt right to hand over the running of the business – and therefore my calling – to someone new who would do things differently and have a bit more energy and resource to throw at it!

Historically, whenever I changed jobs there was always a period of adjusting to the new normal and a new job title comes hand-in-hand with a sense of identity and expectations around it. Typically starting a new role means we have decided to accept an offer of employment. By contrast, the situation I found myself in required an acceptance of my circumstances and reduced capacity, and as a founder stepping down, a 'stepping down' rather than a climbing of a career ladder. And yet it was accompanied by an overwhelming sense of release in being able to hand over the burdens of holding and running the business; where people anticipated reluctance or resentment, I had nothing but relief.

I've noticed that people aspiring to leadership have tended to enquire about how I'd experienced a change in identity around no longer being a CEO and again the only response I have is one of relief. One of the quirks of starting this business has been that I've been entirely (and sometimes quite unhelpfully) blind to job titles: I don't mind what you call my role, I simply know what I need to get on and do to make sure all the plates keep spinning and people don't start shouting at me. It doesn't matter if you want to call me 'MD', 'CEO' or 'Head of Coffee Machine Cleaning' – I just don't want the spinning plates to stop, fall or smash!

So moving out of the role was a real delight as I could stop worrying about the plates, and I'd have a title that would not invite the complaints or approaches of onlookers – that felt like being handed a giant Get Out of Jail Free card. Whilst my email signature says 'Head of Business Development' I've preferred the unofficial title of 'Head of Wining and Dining'!

As this new season of life unfolds, I'm on about a tenth of the caffeine intake I used to be as my body is rather over-sensitive to it these days. I've been intentional about building empty space into my weeks, which has afforded the opportunity to get back to some studying and exploring new activities. Best of all, I've found the great gift of brokenness is that it brings me to an increased dependence on my God who cares for me very greatly indeed. As much as I want to have all the answers at the beginning of the journey, I've had to get comfortable in the not-knowing and to grow in confidence that God will work in His own time. And so, I will hold onto his word:

> See, I am doing a new thing! Now it springs up; do you not perceive it? I am making a way in the wilderness and streams in the wasteland.
> Isaiah 43:19 (NIV)

4

Escape from the past

Ann's story

One of my earliest memories is of standing at my bedroom window watching the city of London burning in the Blitz, before my parents snatched me away to the imagined safety beneath the stairs. Then as stray bombs landed closer and closer to our house, they decided that like so many other Londoners we would also have to evacuate.

We moved to a house in Cambridge, close to all those wonderful old grey stone colleges. But then my mother became seriously ill with cancer and was taken away to a nursing home near my school. I used to visit her every day during break in those last few terrible weeks, but when she died my father took me along to the convent next door, telling me that I would have to stay there whilst he went into hospital himself.

All of life at the convent centred around the chapel, as bells rang endlessly from the Angelus to Benediction. Silent scurrying nuns glided in and out of this peaceful sanctuary at the top of the stairs. When no one else was around I loved to go in there myself. Up here we were level with the top branches of the old cedar trees where grey squirrels played in the shadows. And beside the altar a soft red light glowed permanently, telling me our blessed Lord was there in the sacrament. It was strangely comforting to find myself alone with Him in this peaceful place.

I don't know how long I was there, but one day Sister Anthony took me over to sit by the sundial and said she was going to have to tell me something very difficult to hear. The hospital had rung to say that my father was not going to live through the night and was calling for me to go and say goodbye.

She said that we should look for something to take him, but I could hardly bear to hear the words and the thought that he was leaving me too. That night when they came to tell me he had gone, I felt cold and alone with no one in the whole wide world who cared about me.

I sometimes thought that I would be staying on in the convent with its echoing bells forever, but then one day a couple appeared who had apparently always wanted a little girl of their own. They brought out lovely pictures of the house and garden where they lived and seemed to want me to go and live with them, and suddenly I thought there might be hope for me after all.

Whilst they went off to make all the necessary arrangements, I could hardly contain my excitement, imagining what life would be like in the house I had just seen. In those distant days and especially as it was wartime, there was probably very little examination of how suitable this adoption might be. Besides which, they were personal friends of my godmother which probably gave them the necessary accreditation.

When the time came for me to go and live there it seemed that all my troubles would be far behind me. My new father was a delightful man with a lovely smile and was well known and respected as a director in the film industry at that time. But my mother was often frightening and unpredictable and I never knew what to expect.

As the days went by, I found it incredibly difficult to suddenly become another person with a different name. Time and again they would be hurt if I forgot to call them 'mother' or 'father', not understanding how natural that was.

My father was even deeply hurt if I mentioned the fact that I was adopted, though to this day I have no idea how his friends could fail to observe this! It left me curiously bereft of my own past, as if a part of me had to be cut away forever if I was to be acceptable in my new home.

My new 'mother' proved to be the most volatile of people whose moods swung from one extreme to the other with total unpredictability. She hated Catholicism, and never missed an opportunity to blame the church for anything I got wrong. She seemed to positively flourish on rows and arguments, leaving me reeling from the blows for ages afterwards.

My father's policy was simply to ignore her outbursts of temper completely. 'Don't take any notice,' he would say. 'It's like water off a duck's back; just let it roll off you.' Possibly he could do this, but for me these bitter angry outbursts went straight to the heart and stayed there.

Perhaps there was good reason for her anger as time went by. My father was coming home later and later these days, and whenever I heard his car pull into the drive, I knew that a bitter argument was about to break out in the kitchen just below my bedroom. I felt more and more afraid of life in my unpredictable new 'home'.

One day I found my mother in floods of tears holding a letter in her shaking hands. It seemed that someone was citing my father as co-respondent in a divorce case and that for many months now he had been spending more and more time with another woman – hence the rows when he returned home.

My father made no effort to deny the charges and instead took the opportunity to announce that he was leaving anyway. He too wanted a divorce and would shortly be leaving to go and live with Elizabeth in California. That very night he slammed out of the house leaving me alone to my fate.

Divorce was almost unheard of in those distant days, and the very mention of the word was cause for the most terrible scandal. My mother effectively went to pieces, and I could not help but feel sorry for her. She was almost chain-smoking now and her nicotine-stained hands shook as she tried to cope with the most mundane tasks.

The house was up for sale and my mother's friends helped us settle into a horrible dark little place on the other side of the village. But after that they disappeared from view. Probably even they had had enough of the tears and temper tantrums that occurred almost daily now. Whatever the reason the result was the same – my mother effectively became my sole charge and my responsibility, though I was barely nine years old.

Most of the time it was as if our roles had been reversed and she would call to me pathetically 'Oh Ann, please help me,' which I was happy to do, but it was never enough.

One day she would be slumped in a darkened room, and the next she would be waiting just inside the door, ready to scream at me when I returned from school, for some small mistake I had made. 'Your father would never have left if we had not adopted you!' 'It's all because of you that I have to keep up this house.' And so it went on.

Finally, as my schoolwork ground to a halt, revealing what a struggle I was having, my godmother and the social worker suddenly reappeared on the scene. I was quickly sent away to boarding school, free from my mother's attacks, but already an increasingly unhappy and insecure person on the inside.

This particular school was Church of England, as my mother had taken the opportunity to get me away from the clutches of the Catholic church, as she saw it! However, the terms of the adoption forced her to send me for religious instruction to the old Catholic priest near the school, and this would remain my lifeline during those terrible years. I don't know how much I was able to tell him, but I was always aware of his caring presence and I am sure that he would have been praying for me.

However, he did tell me that although I had to attend the school chapel every day, it was not really a consecrated church or a suitable place to pray! But then again, since I did have to attend their chapel daily, I actually came to love many of the old Anglican hymns and quite often to feel a sense of God's presence, just as often as I did at the Catholic mass up at 'the one true church'.

So here I was suspended between the two denominations, caught in a religious tug-of-war that never ended. Somehow, I survived the next few years and eventually escaped to university as far away as possible, in Scotland. But here again religious divisions began to surface. Catholic friends would get into a terrible state if by any chance they had eaten meat on a Friday or forgotten to go to confession, whereas for Anglicans all this was irrelevant.

By the time I returned home, I had made up my mind to join the ranks of what I thought was a perfectly 'safe' and undemanding denomination. In other words, I would become C of E like everyone else. Something you could just write on a form without any great stir.

However, as the local vicar pointed out, becoming Church of England wasn't just like joining a club, but that there was no point in the exercise unless it involved a personal relationship with God! I listened politely and eventually he accepted my decision, though of course he was absolutely right!

But it was here at church that I met a delightful friend whose parents lived nearby, and who immediately invited me to supper at her flat in London the following week. Several others would be joining us to discuss what was in the Bible. It sounded a bit strange to me, but I really liked her and trusted her judgement.

It turned out to be an exceptional evening with a lovely group of friends who talked about God as if they expected Him to walk in at any moment! I had never known anything like this before, and found myself wishing that I could have the same experience.

I did not have long to wait. One of them asked if they could pray with me, and as they laid hands on me, I had this wonderful experience of God's love flowing through my body. I wanted to cry, the feeling was so beautiful, and so very much what I had needed all those years. As I would soon discover, this love would need to reach down into all the painful caverns of my early years – but that would come later.

The leader of this particular group was a rather good-looking dark haired chap who I admired from a distance. I couldn't have been more astonished than when he asked me out! It turned out that he thought me 'impossibly arty and unconventional!' I was working at the BBC as studio manager and scriptwriter at the time, which probably added to this impression. Despite his first impressions, we were eventually married and settled down happily together close to a thriving church.

Several years later, our vicar announced that he would be starting a counselling course, which sounded really interesting. At this point, I thought of it mainly in terms of being able to help other people, having absolutely no idea of how much I needed this help myself! But even a few days into the course something inside of me was screaming…

Every exercise we were asked to do began to dredge up the terrible experiences of my childhood and I could hardly bear to cope with this. Often, I would return home in floods of tears and my poor husband just could not understand.

'Why on earth do you keep going?' he would ask. It was a valid question, and I did not really know the answer. But somehow, I think I realised that hidden away down here in my memory lay the answer to how I felt about life.

When I told the story of the death of my whole family and the adoption that had gone so badly wrong, in a flat unemotional voice, almost as if it had happened to someone else, one of the group leaders turned to me in amazement. 'I shan't be happy, Ann, until I see you angry about all the things that have happened to you.'

That sounded a very unhelpful and un-Christian remark, but what I didn't realise until later that year, was the fact that shutting out pain shuts out all enjoyment of life as well. If we protect ourselves with this kind of armour-plating, then all the good and happy feelings get barricaded away as well as the bad ones, leaving us in a sort of twilight zone, unable to feel very much at all.

Was this a Pandora's box that I had opened or was it the door to healing as so many on the counselling course had predicted?

Suddenly, out of the blue, two friends from the course offered to come and help me work through some of the deeply buried hurts and memories that I was facing. Their prayerful presence through all of this was invaluable, and I really needed their loving support. I have no idea how long the session lasted, but we had gone back a long way into the mists of time and when it came to an end, I felt totally and utterly exhausted.

But in some strange way, I also felt more alive than I could ever remember feeling! Up until this moment, I had simply accepted each and every blow that life had dealt me with despairing resignation. As a result, my whole horizon had become clouded with hopeless, joyless dust.

Now, God gave me a wonderful new awareness of the beauty of life in full glorious technicolour – almost as if I had never seen it before. The beauty of nature around me, the love of family and friends, the joy of small, everyday things that had previously just washed over me.

But on the other hand, there was of course the very pain that my walls had been designed to keep out! I cried over every sad book and film, and over little things that would scarcely have touched me before.

And as I flooded my way through yet another box of tissues, my poor husband could not really begin to understand what had happened to me. Emotions were something you scarcely ever talked about, let alone expressed in this very un-British fashion!

The extraordinary thing was that I really had no idea that all this was down there. It had effectively been shut out and could only have been recognised by my body language, and the fact that I had always felt so deeply depressed.

I still had a long way to go, but the beginning of this wonderful new freedom from past trauma opened up a much happier future, and more importantly, the ability to help other hurting people around me find healing and escape.

> Yet to all who received him, to those who believed in his name, He gave the right to become children of God – children born not of natural descent, nor of human decision or of a husband's will, but born of God.
> John 1:12–13 (NIV)

> For I have learnt to be content whatever the circumstances. I know what it is to be in need and I know what it is to have plenty. I have learnt the secret of being content in any and every situation, whether well fed or hungry, whether living in plenty or in want. I can do everything through him who gives me strength.
> Philippians 4:11–13 (NIV)

5

Brokenness builds a bridge

Elaine's story

The only thing I ever remembered about the accident was that the car I'd hit was red.

Other than that, my mind was just a blank about what'd happened. I was in a hospital bed, leg in traction, in and out of consciousness. Later on, different people told me they'd been to visit me but I had no memory of them. Others had walked straight past my bed, unable to recognise me because of the state of my face, or saw me, felt sick and faint with the shock and had to recover before they could come back to see me.

The nurses didn't give me a mirror and I had no idea what I looked like, nor do I think I even cared about my appearance in those early days. My nose had been flattened as my face hit the steering wheel. It had to be rebuilt with plastic surgery. My legs were both broken, my femur shattered and I'd lost a lot of blood.

I was 23, returning home from work after a day's teaching and my life had changed forever. It transpired that I had crashed into another teacher, who herself was returning from school, in a high speed collision. We never found out how the accident had been caused, though one of us must have crossed the central line on the country road we were on. Her children were in the car and were uninjured, and her daughter bravely ran to the nearest farmhouse to ring for help. We were put in side-by-side beds in hospital and used to pray together across the beds, as we found out we were both Christians. It took a year from then to be able to go back to work full-time and I've rarely been able to walk without pain since that day.

When you're already riddled with poor self-worth and insecurity and you find you can no longer do what everyone else can do, it feels like an open door to a greater degree of worthlessness.

But where did the low sense of self-esteem start? It's hard to know exactly. I was a planned and wanted baby, the second child of a young married Christian couple. I had a brother 18 months older than me with whom I had a really close relationship, which was great. But there were many times in my childhood when I felt insecure and unlovable, as though I was trying to live up to a standard I couldn't reach. I think I just didn't quite fit in, thought my own thoughts and opinions were unimportant, and felt that I wasn't quite good enough to be acceptable. Through time I became a people-pleaser to make other people's lives as easy as possible, taking responsibility for bad atmospheres and uncomfortable emotions so others experienced as little discomfort as possible, regardless of the impact on me.

Through my childhood and teenage years, I held onto the core belief that you couldn't show anyone what really went on inside your head. My church at the time was not a place where people shared testimonies and no one aired their problems in public. Maybe this was a British thing of the time, a stiff-upper-lip mentality. Google tells me that this was often valued as a sign of dignity and strength, showing fortitude in the face of adversity, but in reality, it was just a mask I wore to hide what was really going on inside from the rest of the world. At that time, we wore our 'Sunday best' for church and looked like wonderful, sorted and saintly beings! But that wasn't who I was.

So, since the crash, what were the results of being physically limited and carrying a load of emotional damage? I used to tell myself that I was just rubbish, that no one likes me because I'm just a burden. I was worried about what others thought of me. I thought that everyone just saw my inability to walk well as my own fault. I thought I'd function better if I was a different version of myself – thinner, fitter, more disciplined, all-round a more together person, whatever that looks like. If I was like that then I'd be worth knowing and spending time with.

I spent many years allowing others to make decisions for me about what I could and couldn't do, especially around my ability to walk, when those decisions should have been mine to make. I'd wanted people to know where I needed help without actually voicing what would help me, and then felt let down by them, even though I hadn't asked for help, when I took on tasks that left me in considerable pain for many hours after, so that even the thought of getting up to make myself a drink or go to the bathroom filled me with dread. It felt like there was a part of me that was crying out to be seen and known but was too insecure to voice what would've helped me.

So where did my healing start?

I gave my life to God at the age of 14 when challenged about whether or not I would be going to heaven if I died that night. I didn't tell my parents what I'd done but they saw a difference in me from that moment. It was the start of a very long process of healing and correcting of my thought-life. My insecurities had led me to do some stupid things as a teenager, even though I knew they were wrong. I'd just wanted to feel loved. I'd also had times of depression where I just didn't want to wake up the next morning and prayed that I would wake up dead. Fortunately, God chose to say no to that prayer!

In my second year of university, I had one of those moments in my life when my thinking shifted. I'd just started going to a new church and went to a home group where someone was giving their life story. This lady was talking about sleeping with boyfriends and having had to have an abortion before she had become a Christian. I couldn't believe she was being so open about her past, especially in front of people she had never met before – I was flabbergasted!

I was also undone by it. She was clearly comfortable doing this. Plus no one in the room looked shocked or disgusted by what she'd done. They looked like this was just a normal part of a journey into a life with God. I'd never encountered the like of this before and it changed me. Maybe it was actually okay to let down your guard from time to time?

Years later, God would give me the phrase 'Brokenness builds a bridge' and I would see so much benefit in sharing my struggles with others as a key part of building relationships. I have since found that authenticity and honesty form the best connections in genuine friendships with other people, especially with other lovers of God who can encourage you, support and pray for you when you go through challenges or simply when you want to find His healing.

Through all this, God has been healing me on the inside. I've been like Shrek, a green ogre who has layers, and God has faithfully dismantled layer after layer to bring me the emotional healing that I need. I'm not completely there yet but He is absolutely on my case.

I ask God on a fairly regular basis to heal me and I invite Him into the darkest parts of my being. Psalm 51:10 NIV sums this up when it says, 'Create in me a pure heart, O God and renew a steadfast spirit within me.' It's up to Him to do this work, not me. It doesn't say, 'Help me create in myself a clean heart'. I can't do it myself. He's so kind, He brings things to light bit by bit, so I'm not overwhelmed by the scale of stuff He wants to deal with.

I've also been learning about the power of my words. I used to curse myself with what I would say about myself, calling myself 'stupid' or 'useless' and the like. But the Bible says, 'The power of life and death is in the tongue' (Proverbs 18:21) and I refuse to speak those things out over myself any more. I don't get it right all the time but I'm trying to only say what God says about me.

I've found the Holy Spirit is the most amazing teacher and leader. He's led me to Bible passages, to friends, to online teachings and to conferences that have brought me healing and also, my favourite, to moments of experiencing His presence with me in a life-changing way. Once I was really struggling and I was listening to a recording of a prophetic conference while sorting through clothes in my bedroom. The lady who was speaking said that if you needed to respond to the message you should stand up where you were. So, half-dressed as I'd being trying on different bits of clothing, I stood up and God's presence flooded through me. His presence with me was really palpable and He did something in the core of me which changed me and brought another degree of His healing.

Every time I encounter Him, He brings me healing. At a conference with my Void 2 Value co-host Ro, I went to the front because I needed prayer and the Holy Spirit firstly knocked me out and then, just like at Pentecost when the Holy Spirit first came, I was drunk under His power and laughed and laughed and laughed very loudly for several hours. I was unable to walk straight and staggered to the carpark by holding onto the wall. It was the most amazing feeling. I felt so loved. Plus, there is no hangover after a Holy Spirit encounter! On leaving the building, I was still laughing and had to hold onto the wall to walk to the carpark and in the car, I was completely unable to help Ro with the navigation because I couldn't stop giggling and I didn't care what direction she was driving.

So where am I now? I still walk with a limp and am often in pain, but I am in a very different place of knowing who I am and what God really thinks about me. The internal healing has been remarkable. I've had other moments with Him where joy has come over me and I've been able to laugh even in really tough circumstances. It's felt like bubbles coming up on the inside and it has definitely been a God thing – I love it!

My relationships are so much better. They are based on honesty and frank conversation rather me just saying what I think people want to hear. I am so much more confident in God's love for me and my value to Him. I've realised He never leaves me, not even in my muddled, faithless days when I fall apart or when I allow ungodly thoughts to have space in my head.

In the past I believed somewhere deep inside me that these were all things that would push Him away but I know now His incredible kindness and faithfulness to me. Coming to God in my most broken state, telling Him the truth about what's going on inside and letting Him sort me out has got me out of the pit of worthlessness and insecurity and onto the solid ground of His incredible love.

> I waited patiently for the LORD;
> he turned to me and heard my cry.
> He lifted me out of the slimy pit,
> out of the mud and mire;
> he set my feet on a rock
> and gave me a firm place to stand.
> He put a new song in my mouth,
> a hymn of praise to our God.
> Many will see and fear the LORD
> and put their trust in him.
> Psalm 40:1–3 (NIV)

6

Perfectionism is a curse

Kevin's story

Perfectionism is something which doesn't just happen. I believe it is something formed in us from a young age for various reasons. The purpose of this chapter is to share how I believe perfectionism sneakily became an integral part of my identity from a young age and the way in which God helped me get free from it.

I grew up in the Northwest Highlands of Scotland which, you may be aware, is a religious melting pot in the United Kingdom. Although my Scottish mother had been raised Church of Scotland, my father was an Irish Roman Catholic and my mother even had to take Roman Catholic vows to be able to marry my father. Therefore, I and my three older brothers were raised Roman Catholic and sent to Catholic school from age five.

I think it was during my time in Catholic school that my performance mindset and perfectionism tendencies began to be formed. For example, every Monday morning at school the teacher would stand at the front of class and ask the question, 'Who did not go to Mass yesterday?' Being honest, I would raise my hand. As a five-year-old child (in the late '70s) I would then be asked to come forward where I would be belted, with a forked leather belt in front of the entire class. This was a shocking and traumatic experience. Sadly, this would be a common occurrence which I tried to get out of but with little success.

My father worked away from home Monday to Friday building roads (typical stereotype of an Irishman). Therefore, when he came home at the weekends, he would enjoy spending time with his family and taking his two younger boys fishing. I remember explaining to my parents what happened at school and how I was belted for not going to Mass. They didn't believe me. My older brothers told them the same, as they were also regularly belted for not going to Mass, but they were not believed either; they just seemed to accept the punishment from the teachers each week.

My parents didn't force me to go to Mass, to be honest; they didn't really care. The nuns and priests in the surrounding area who were linked with the school and would visit from time to time were all great. It was just the teachers who wielded their power as hyper-religious authoritarians causing great pain and turmoil to the pupils.

I remember begging my dad to let us go to Mass on our way to fishing so I wouldn't be belted on Monday at school. He had no issue with this. Unfortunately, we turned up late for Mass and sat at the back. The next day at school, the teacher would ask her usual Monday morning question, 'Who never went to Mass yesterday?' I would keep my hand down as I had gone to Mass.

'Brogan!' I was shocked to hear my name called out. 'Did you go to Mass yesterday?' 'Yes,' I answered. 'Which Mass?' she asked. '9am, St Anne's.' 'That's funny!', she exclaimed. 'I was at 9am St Anne's and I didn't see you there.' 'I was sitting at the back with my dad and brother,' I explained. She would then ask, 'What colour of garment was the priest wearing?' 'I don't know' – I never paid attention and was only a small boy. 'What Gospel did the priest read from?' she then asked. 'I don't know.' I would then be dragged from my seat to the front and belted in front of everyone. Whether I had gone to Mass or not made no difference, I would be belted.

Thankfully, a few years later, Margaret Thatcher abolished corporal punishment in the schools and we could no longer be belted. The teachers, however, found other ways to punish children who did not attend Mass. They would still ask their usual Monday morning question, 'Who didn't go to Mass yesterday?' However, instead of calling pupils out to the front to be belted, they would call them out to be quizzed and ridiculed. I remember being called out one time, after being accused of not attending Mass, where I was asked, 'How many hours are in a day? Write it on the blackboard.' I wrote '24'.

I would then be asked, 'How many days are in a week? Write it on the blackboard.' I wrote '7'. 'How many hours are in a week? Write it on the blackboard.' By this time, I would have to do a multiplication sum in front of the entire class to eventually come up with the correct answer of 168 hours, being ridiculed in the process. Once the correct answer was calculated and written on the board, the teacher would then go into a guilt tirade saying things like, 'There are 168 hours in a week, and God only requires one hour of your time to go to Mass, and you don't go! You are a naughty child, and you are going to burn in hell!'

This constant barrage of abuse directed at me at a young age, highlighted an angry God who needed to be appeased by religious obedience – which I now know not to be true. In the end, the only way I could get out of being abused verbally at school was to become an altar boy and serve at one of the weekend Masses.

When I was ten years old, sadly my father, who at the time was only forty-five years old, died of a heart attack, leaving my mother a young widow, having to raise four boys on her own. This tragedy was traumatic for us all and hit me hard. It cast us as a family into poverty which was worrying for my mother, needing to make ends meet with such a young family and such responsibility.

While serving as an altar boy at my own father's funeral I was so distraught that I had to leave during the service and go into the vestry (sacristy) until the service was over. I remember my mum coming to check on me and I was crying. I asked the priest at this time, 'How could God allow my father to die at such a young age and what was I to do now?' Something bizarre then took place which I will never forget as long as I live. The priest explained to me that my father was in purgatory, and it was my job to pray for him so he could get to heaven.

I asked what I needed to do. He said I needed to pray the Lord's Prayer for my father every day so he can get to heaven. I asked, 'How long for?'; he said 'For the rest of your life.' I asked what would happen if I forgot, and what if I don't. He responded, 'then your father will not get to heaven, and it would be your fault!' Clearly this distressed me – remember this was on the day of my father's funeral, and here I am as a 10-year-old boy trying to come to grips with this misfortune of my father dying which had been thrust upon me, and asking for some simple clarification.

I realised when I became a Christian eight years later that what the priest had told me was both untrue and unbiblical. His theology was based on Christ's sacrifice on the cross not being enough and we as humans having to play our own part towards the forgiveness of sin in addition to Jesus' part. Thankfully, Christ's sacrifice was enough and in Paul's letter to the Ephesians he explains this beautifully:

> For by grace you have been saved through faith; and that not of yourselves, it is the gift of God: not as a result of works, so that no one may boast.
> Ephesians 2:8–9 (NASB 1995)

Although I attended the Roman Catholic church religiously until the end of primary school (age 12), after primary school I stopped attending. However, I did religiously pray the Lord's Prayer for my father every night before going to bed until I was about 14 years of age, when I became quite rebellious and stopped.

Despite my rebelliousness and ups and downs as a teenager, I managed to finish high school with most of my grades. I left home at 16 which broke my mother's heart (as I was the youngest, I expect) and I moved away to start a four-year apprenticeship. It was during this time that I became a born-again Christian at 18 years of age through a radical encounter with God (which would be a complete chapter in this book in itself). I was working in a hotel kitchen where the chef continually told me about Jesus, about the truth of the gospel. I met people on the street doing church outreach which impacted me even if I didn't stop to listen.

When people were giving me the gospel, God brought to my remembrance Bible stories and Bible verses I had heard as a child in the Roman Catholic church. Thankfully He wastes nothing! Through His grace and faithfulness, He made it possible for me to find my way to Him and I asked Him to forgive me for my sins and come into my life.

I should have enjoyed my new-found salvation, which I probably did for the first year or two. Sadly, then the legalism that I had been brought up with began to kick in. I became religious with my Bible readings and prayers, thinking that if I had not read my Bible today or not spoken to God today in prayer then He would be cross with me, just as I'd been told He was always cross with me in Catholic school for not going to Mass. If I had met my religious standards then I would feel good about myself but if I had not, then my tainted view of God made me believe He was angry with me as I had not performed to His standard (which in fact was my standard).

This is not a good place to be in. God loves us for who we are to Him, not for what we do for Him. I am reminded of Paul's letter to the Galatians:

> It was for freedom that Christ set us free; therefore keep standing firm and do not be subject again to a yoke of slavery. Galatians 5:1 (NASB 1995)

After my apprenticeship I undertook a five-year Master's Degree in Mechanical Engineering which I completed in four years (which is only achieved by one in 150 students per year). For every piece of coursework, every presentation, every exam I would give over and above what was required. I would serve in the church, attend all the meetings, read the Bible and pray religiously. However, my life was out of balance as I would always seem to be stressed out; nothing was ever good enough for my perfectionist standards and legalistic nature. Although I had a deep love for God and I experienced His love daily, my own misgivings and the false lies I had been believing about God the Father were detrimental to my physical, mental and emotional well-being.

At age 30 I had become a Chartered Engineer. Despite my often 'warped' view of God, my religiosity and my legalistic nature, I did have a close relationship with Him. He took me on amazing adventures of faith with Him and at age 36 I had become the pastor of a church which He called my wife and I to start. Within a few years the church had grown so much that I stopped engineering altogether and worked full-time for the church. Even during this time perfectionism caused me to be so inefficient that I would be working over 70 hours a week, though I was only supposed to work 40 hours. This was due to spending too much time on sermons, taking ages to answer emails to perfection, and so on. My strength was that I was very pastoral with people, and I knew they experienced God's love through me; my weakness was spending copious amounts of time, due to perfectionism, on things that really weren't that important.

It was in 2015 that God challenged me to take on a full-time theology and Christian leadership course (online) while still pastoring full-time. With my perfectionism mindset this was an impossibility for me to undertake but God clearly knew what He was doing; He wanted to break this debilitating mindset, and this was

His way of doing exactly that. I remember Him explaining to me one time about what I now call the 80/20 rule (which I have since used to help a lot of people who struggle with perfectionism as I did).

In essence, if we assume something should take one hour to complete, then as a perfectionist it would take me one hour to complete 80 per cent of the work and then another four hours or so to perfect the final 20 per cent, which was not actually that important. What should have taken one hour would take me five hours. Due to my limited time, and with the coursework I had to do, I really sensed God challenge me to put in 80 per cent of the work then leave the final 20 per cent, i.e. the perfectionist part. This was so challenging for me but became life-changing.

My sermons became more relatable. My stress levels dropped, and I became less intense and began to enjoy life more. I stopped worrying about all the things that could go wrong and stopped trying to control things. My wife and kids said I changed overnight, all because God forced me into a situation where I had to leave perfectionism behind. My personal relationship with God became transformed and I began to see Him as a Father instead of a taskmaster.

When meditating on the grace and unconditional love of the Father-heart of God, I often wonder what father would be upset if his child fell asleep in his arms when speaking to him. Our heavenly father is the same. We think we are letting God down if we fall asleep while we pray (as I sometimes do), but He is just delighted to have His son or daughter in His arms. We need to see God differently. It is not about performance, or being transactional, it is about relationship.

When we look at Paul's letter to the Galatians, they had been set free but preferred to approach God on their religious terms. That is exactly what I did. I had been set free but reverted back to my perfectionist and legalistic ways. We therefore need to remind ourselves of the verse I mentioned earlier:

> It was for freedom that Christ set us free; therefore keep standing firm and do not be subject again to a yoke of slavery. Galatians 5:1 (NASB 1995)

You are unconditionally loved and accepted by Him because of who you are, not because of what you do. Praise God!

7

How to be when you can't be busy

Kim's story

What do you do when at age 26 your body suddenly ceases to let you be the busy, activity-loving person that you used to be? When all the church, social and outdoor activities you love become impossible and even the garden is out of reach? When horizontal in bed is the only place you can be and even getting up for the bathroom can mean horizontal on the floor instead? Well, the simple answer to that part is to get a commode and in your early 30s learn about the indignities of life! It also makes you think of all the folk who have had to live like that their entire lives so, 'How can I complain?'

Hardest of all though was the loss of a busy, fulfilling life and the companionship of friends who were too busy to visit. Friendships were based around activities with them, being at church, meeting at the school gates and having play get-togethers with your respective offspring. But ongoing sickness, where sound and light were often unbearable and gastric symptoms were frequent, didn't fit with all this. My 'busyness' now was suddenly needing to work out through the pain and a foggy brain how I was going to meet the basic necessities of my beautiful child – food, clean clothes, getting to school and, most of all, to know she was still loved by a mum who was suddenly unable 'to do' anything.

However, this isn't the place to go into details of the practical solutions I had to find, such as finding carers for me. Enough to note that some were helpful, but others were very much out of my control and hard to bear, adding to the distress of unremitting illness symptoms affecting my whole body. More relevant is how did I get through the hours of unwelcome solitude, not knowing what was happening to my once active body or how long it would go on. How could I possibly 'be' without being busy?

There were no mobile phones, the landline was attached to the wall and the internet only available to a few, and then you couldn't make or receive a phone call whilst using it anyway. I sound ancient but, let's remember, technology has moved fast over the last four decades! So, I had a lot of time alone, in pain and unable to sit up for more than a few minutes. Thankfully there was one Companion who didn't need technology to communicate with me, didn't ask me questions I couldn't answer and, of utmost importance to me, didn't seem offended by my condition.

It didn't make the very real suffering any easier though, but God led me to Bible passages that I would once have skipped uncomfortably over – notably Job. Who wants to think about the awful things he went through and, oh yes, God allowed it! However, when life seems inexplicably distressing it is so very helpful that God had Job's story put in His written word! For all I knew, there could be a spiritual battle going on for my life too.

Just briefly, I had difficult times in my childhood when adults took me along to unholy meetings in worship of the enemy. I'm sure therefore this enemy of our souls thought he had ownership of me and how mad would he have been when I gave my life to Jesus at age 13. Therefore, when I looked at Job properly it gave me encouragement that God would only allow the enemy to go so far and no more. My life was in His hands and no-one could ever snatch me from them (John 10:28).

I always knew that God was well aware of my situation because at the age of 16 I had been given a word from Him by a godly man in my church. God said that I was entering a long dark tunnel which would be hard, but that He would never leave me, although at times it may feel that He had. I was to trust Him in it and through it. I asked, 'How long will the tunnel be?' The godly man wept as he said, 'I believe God is letting you know it will be very long; but you will come out into the light.' This may seem a hard thing to some, that God should give such a troubling word to a 16-year-old, and I've had responses to that effect on the rare occasions I've shared it.

However, firstly, I had already begun to enter that frighteningly dark tunnel and so it was strangely comforting to have my Heavenly Father talk to me about it. Particularly as part of the reason for feeling the tunnel walls closing around me was the shock at how my earthly father had turned on me in anger and disgust when I gave my life to Jesus. Even though I sought to just quietly go to church, not talking to him about it because of his strong atheistic views, he treated me with a contempt that made life at home wretched. The loss of the close relationship we'd had was devastating. Secondly, my Heavenly Father's word to me is what kept me going through that long period of my life, where many things caused great darkness in the depths of that tunnel.

Knowing that God cared so deeply for me that He had forewarned me, and assured me that He would be with me the whole time, was so much more important than it is possible to explain here. It also reminded me of Jesus's words:

> I have told you these things, so that in me you may have peace. In the world you will have trouble. But take heart! I have overcome the world. John 16:33 (NIV)

I still didn't know the reason why I had to go through this, nor why it had to last for years, but what a difference it made having that word from God my Heavenly Father. Peter tells us:

> Though now for a little while you may have had to suffer grief in all kinds of trials. These have come so that the proven genuineness of your faith – of greater worth than gold, which perishes even though refined by fire – may result in praise, glory and honour when Jesus Christ is revealed. 1 Peter 1:6–7 (NIV)

How great is the second verse, but those words 'for a little while' would likely have been troublesome to me if God himself hadn't told me my trials would be long ones!

Some had suggested I must have unforgiven sin to remain so ill, but God didn't say that and believe me, I checked with Him! Others said there must be unforgiveness from me towards someone, but God knew there wasn't. He'd led me through the difficult and long task of forgiving those who had dragged me along to those unholy meetings, as well as other more minor but niggling things we have to forgive as we go through life!

Here in Job He was reassuring me my illness wasn't my fault, which was sadly implied by a few 'Job's comforters' I had the misfortune to have occasional visits from. One even asked me why I wasn't angry with God. Angry with Him? He was the only one truly comforting and upholding me in this new 'can't-be-busy' life.

Therefore, it was vitally important to me to know that God knew why I could no longer be busy, and of course He did, and He cared that I was having unremitting distressing things happen to my body. I knew it in my heart and from reading His word which tells us He sees even the sparrow that falls (Matthew 10:29). Of course I questioned Him! Having dealt with, 'Is it because of something I've done or not done Lord?', and hearing His *'No!'* get louder with every well-meaning person who said otherwise, I moved onto 'Lord, wasn't I of more value to You when I could get to church twice on Sunday, play in the worship group, sing in the choir, lead Sunday school?' His still small voice came back, 'No, my child, often you were too busy to meet properly with Me.'

I knew then, deep in my soul, that what He valued most was intimacy with me. My life wasn't the gaping void that sometimes felt like it was going to swallow me up; even in the dire circumstances of that time I was of immense value to God because He had created me to be in relationship with Him.

However, the horrible symptoms of the illness and not knowing what my prognosis was, the loss of social life and ability to be the active mum I had wanted to be, still took their toll. At times I became very depressed, even to the point of wondering whether my family would be better off without me. Maybe it would be the kindest thing for them to be free of me and this awful illness, and I wouldn't have to suffer any more? During one particularly dark time I needed reassurance that my life wasn't meaningless and of no value because I couldn't do the things I used to. It took all my physical strength to lift my Bible and try and read it from a lying down position, but it felt urgent to try.

I couldn't think about reading plans or anything like that; I was just desperate to know if His word had anything in it that could help me right then. Struggling to hold it (remember, no lightweight electronic devices way back then!), I read where it opened:

> This day I call the heavens and the earth as witnesses against you that I have set before you life and death, blessings and curses. Now choose life, so that you and your children may live and that you may love the LORD

your God, **listen to his voice, and hold fast to him.** For the LORD is your life.
Deuteronomy 30:19,20 (NIV) (bold mine)

Wow! Only it wasn't exactly 'Wow' I felt back then, more 'But Lord, it's so hard when living like this is just horrible.' But He also gave me Psalm 118:17 (NIV) and encouraged me to keep declaring it: 'I will not die but live, and will proclaim what the LORD has done.

Sometimes it was with reluctance when things were really tough, but knowing God had led me to those passages in His word I chose life and kept choosing it every time God nudged me to. Did I get better? No, not at all at that time, and I didn't have any sense that choosing life would bring about my healing then. It was just vital to make that choice and trust God with the rest of my life, however it may look. It seemed strange to some that I never thought 'Why me?', but more, 'Why *not* me?', because bad things happen to ordinary people.

A sad fact that often added to my distressing circumstances is that society often equates being of value with being busy, and even more sadly this attitude is often rife in the church too. Therefore, when God gave me His peace that passes understanding, despite my circumstances (Philippians 4:7), the world and even some in the church thought this was somehow wrong and brought me much condemnation for accepting a situation I couldn't change!

Of course I had asked God to heal me, to stop the suffering, to let me do the things I had thought were important to Him. But I again remembered His message to me at the young age of 16 and rested in the knowledge that He knew and that there was a reason. I was also reassured by Paul's testimony: his thorn in the flesh (2 Corinthians 12:8–10) may not be explicit but imagine the ongoing pain and irritation that it describes. Yet God did not relieve him of it but instead promised: 'My strength is made perfect in weakness.' 2 Corinthians 12:9 (NIV).

However, Ephesians goes on to say: 'For we are God's handiwork, created in Christ Jesus to do good works, which God prepared in advance for us to do.' Ephesians 2:10 (NIV).

So, are we suddenly valueless to Him when we can't be busy? That isn't what He taught me through those long periods of enforced inactivity. God's work is not to be equated with 'busyness' and will never be burdensome, because He promised 'My yoke is easy and my burden is light.' (Matthew 11:30) My 'work' then was to trust Him, to ask Him to help me manage the essentials of life, family and home in the middle and muddle of it all. He did.

I was also given the gift of a cross-stitch kit – me who had always hated sewing and the sitting involved in it! But it was a time to consider new things and ways of doing life, and at times the challenge brought a sense of fulfilment. I found that in short periods and from a semi-reclined position I could make simple, but meaningful, cross-stitch items to give to people – minor but meaningful.

Of course, God needs people to carry out His purposes on earth, to be His hands and feet, but if the Christian life for you means being busy, are you keeping a check on what is of God and what isn't? I ask this because, well, I'm writing this nearly 40 years after the illness first knocked me off my feet and I'm much improved from those first devastating years of having to be permanently horizontal. Now, I can sometimes be busy! God has given me a 'mission field' among other people with various disabilities who don't do church, and to encourage churches to become accessible so that those who don't go now could if they wanted to! I can now see how those difficult and at times distressing experiences have honed what I learnt in my earlier, relatively short spell of previous training and work, with folk with complex needs, before becoming ill. No-one can quite understand situations as well as someone else who has been, or is, in a similar one!

However, I'm still limited in how much I can do and how long I can be upright and therefore still learning 'how to be when you can't be busy'. In writing this chapter, I began to feel pensive, realising that as my health now allows me to be busy at times, I can so easily forget. Forget the important thing God taught me in those 'unable to be busy years'.

He desires foremost our undivided attention, our hearts and our love. I believe the story John tells about Martha and Mary (Luke 10:38–42) is of immense importance because it shows there is often a choice to be busy or not. I know I can easily be a 'Martha' and get resentful, especially because I tire and can relapse into worse illness symptoms very easily. I'm so grateful God had this event included in His word! How beautiful that Jesus said Mary had chosen the better part of sitting at His feet listening to Him. Chosen!

So, there was no guilt for Mary who chose not to be busy at that time. And there was no guilt for Job who had no choice, but God knew exactly the position he was in and, most importantly, why. God restored all things and more to him. Although I am still limited by illness and disability, He has done this in many ways for me and whether in this life or when I go to be with Him or He returns, I will be restored to full health – healing will come. For now, I echo Paul's words in Romans 8:18: 'For I consider that our present sufferings are not worth comparing with the glory that will be revealed in us.'

Occasionally, I catch myself looking back at the times I was very ill, when I was unable to be busy at all, and for a moment fear starts to descend. Then He reminds me that He was with me then, is with me each moment in the 'now', and He will be with me each day of my future – because that will simply become the 'now' too.

As an encouragement for those who may relate to my journey, I want to share that my daughter, in spite of everything we went through together and all she went through because of my illness, has turned into a beautiful, balanced and emotionally healthy woman who, in her late thirties gave her life to Christ. Since emerging from the darkness of that tunnel a few years ago, my happiest moment was being able to fully enter into the joy of her baptism!

As for me, I am rejoicing at being back in the light with no tunnel walls around me. Is life perfect? Of course not! I still have to deal daily with managing chronic illness, disability, the stigma it can bring, and watching my beautiful daughter struggle with the same inherited conditions. But there are also wonderful times when I can whizz around town in my electric wheelchair – it is truly wonderful feeling the wind in your hair after being confined to bed for a very long time! – or explore the beauty of the countryside, and visit friends. Times when I can go into my garden, feed the fish and the wild but characterful birds, enjoy the beauty of the flowers and fruits. And He is with me in all of it: the difficult, the wonderful and the in-between!

8

Following the butterfly

Kenny's story

I never thought I'd be the guy with a testimony about escaping cartels and hearing God's voice on a mountain. I mean, I believed in God, sure, but I wasn't what you'd call religious. I was just a touring event guy who worked with big artists, tried to stay in shape, and wanted to get home to my wife and kids.

But sometimes God shows up in the most unlikely places. For me, it was on a rocky mountainside in Mexico, broken and bleeding, with armed men hunting me.

It was 23 August 2024. I was on tour with the Jonas Brothers in Monterrey, Mexico. Just another work trip. I'd been doing this for over 20 years travelling the world, working backstage with massive productions. It was my dream career.

I'd worked hard to stay healthy on the road while most tour guys burned out. I was actually on day 14 of the mental toughness programme called '75 Hard' when this incident happened. Part of it required two 45-minute workouts every day, one of them outdoors. So that evening, around 6pm, on our evening off, I decided to hike up the trail I could see from my hotel room. It looked safe enough, locals were using it like a commuter path – families, workers, kids. I just wanted to do a quick hike up to get some photos of the valley and finish my workout. What could go wrong, right?

So, I'm walking along this dirt road at the top, taking pictures, feeling pretty good about life. Then this dirt bike style motorcycle pulls right up next to me. Two guys, yelling in Spanish, making motions like they want my phone. My gut immediately said, 'This is not good.' I tried to play dumb, pointed at my headphones, as if to say, 'I'm just out for a hike.' And kept walking. But then one guy jumped off the bike and started coming at me. The other picked up a boulder and threw it at my head.

That's when I started running. Another rock was thrown at my head and it caused me to trip. I looked back and two more motorcycles with two guys apiece on them were headed in my direction on the dirt road.

I heard the first gunshot maybe a minute later. They were shooting at me! I realised, this isn't a robbery. These guys aren't going to let me live and I'm not about to let them take me. I had two toddlers at home and a wife who needed me. In that split second, I made a decision that saved my life and definitely changed it forever.

I jumped off the mountain. The impact snapped my femur. I heard my leg bone break, and screamed, 'I've got kids!' as I rolled another thirty feet into a cactus. I collapsed again and as I rolled another fifteen feet down the mountain, my left arm broke and I slammed into a thorn bush. I'd never broken a bone in my life. Now I had two major breaks and was covered in cactus spines, bleeding, unable to walk. The pain was unlike anything I'd ever experienced.

I could hear those motorcycles above me. The guys started to search the mountainside and were hunting me. This is where my story stops being about survival skills and becomes about something I can't explain away. I was hiding in this dense thorn bush, terrified, in agony, thinking I might die on that mountain. And I cried out, 'God, please. If you want me to live, Lord, please tell me what to do.'

That's when a hummingbird flew right in front of my face and started feeding on a flower in the bush. For just a moment, in all that chaos and fear, I saw beauty. I thought, 'Thank you, God. This is beautiful.' And in the same moment, I thought, 'God, you are such a comedian. Please, Lord, if you want me to live, show me what to do!'

At that moment a butterfly flew right by my left ear, and I heard this loud, clear voice: 'Follow the butterfly!' I'm not the kind of guy who hears voices. I'm pretty practical, pretty grounded. But I heard that voice as clearly as I'm telling you this story now.

I got some divine strength and painfully dragged my broken body into an even denser thorn bush about ten feet in front of me. The butterfly landed inside the thorn bush and I curled up right next to it and got quiet. About a minute later, one of the cartel guys came around the bush I was just hiding in…he didn't see me.

That butterfly wasn't afraid of me at all. It just sat there, like it was meant to be there. Like God had sent it.

What happened next was twelve hours of the hardest thing I've ever done. I had to drag my broken body down that mountain in complete darkness, staying hidden in thorn bushes while those guys hunted me throughout the night.

Every time I thought I couldn't go any further, every time I wanted to give up, I'd get a vision, like a download in my mind, showing me how to get past whatever obstacle was in front of me. A rock pile. A bundle of sticks. A tree blocking my path. Then I'd hear that voice again: 'Keep moving forward!' And somehow, I'd find the strength to keep going.

God gave me gifts along the way. A perfectly shaped rock that fit my hand like it was made for me, protecting my palm as I dragged myself over the rocks. A five-gallon bucket that appeared right when I needed to get around a tree. A plastic bin that became a sled for the final stretch. These weren't coincidences. God was providing exactly what I needed, when I needed it.

The closest I came to giving up wasn't from the physical pain, it was when they came back with dogs. I was lying in a thin thorn bush, completely exposed, watching flashlight beams sweep over the mountain. I could hear one of the men breathing, maybe ten feet away from me. I could hear his dog.

I covered the white logo on my shirt with my hands and prayed harder than I'd ever prayed in my life. 'God, please don't let them find me. Please don't let them see me.' And somehow…somehow, they walked the other way.

I lay there for forty-five minutes in complete shock. How did they not see me? How did that dog not smell me? That's when I made a promise to God. 'If you get me through this, if you let me live, I'll give you my life. Whatever you want me to do, Lord, I will do it.'

After twelve hours of crawling, I finally made it to the street level. A young guy walking to work saw me and got help from my hotel. When they loaded me into the hotel SUV, I knew I'd made it. I was alive. But here's the thing about God's rescue, it wasn't just about getting off that mountain. The real work was just beginning. The physical recovery was tough. Hip replacement surgery and months of physical therapy, learning to walk again. But the emotional recovery nearly broke me.

A few months later, I fell into a deep depression. I was angry, short with my family, pulling away from everyone. I didn't understand why God had saved me if I was just going to feel this lost and dark. I started having thoughts I'd never had before. Dark thoughts. I told my wife I was scared, that I didn't know who I was any more.

That's when God met me again, this time in a physical therapy office. My therapist's assistant, Evelyn, invited me to visit her church to see her get baptised. Something in my heart just broke open, and I asked if I could be baptised too.

On 24 January 2025, I went under that water and came up a different man. The darkness was gone. Just like on the mountain, it was supernatural. You see, God doesn't always remove the mountain. Sometimes He meets you in the drag down it.

I learned that God's voice isn't always gentle and quiet. Sometimes it's loud and commanding… 'Keep moving forward!' And sometimes it comes through a butterfly that shows up exactly when you need guidance. I learned that God provides, but not always in ways that make sense. A rock, a bucket, a plastic bin – these became instruments of His rescue.

Most importantly, I learned that surrender isn't weakness. When I stopped trying to figure everything out and started trusting God's guidance, that's when I found real strength. Not the kind that comes from my own effort, but the kind that flows through me when I'm connected to something bigger than myself.

I think about the verse, 'I can do all things through Christ who strengthens me.' Philippians 4:13 (NIV)

Not because I'm strong, but because He is strong in me. Not because I had all the answers, but because I learned to follow the butterfly, to trust His guidance even when it doesn't make sense.

Here's what I know…Your mountain is coming, if it hasn't come already. And here's what I know now through it all…you're not climbing it alone. God meets us in the mess. He provides what we need. He gives us strength to keep moving forward and sometimes, if we ask for His help, He sends a butterfly to show us the way.

To discover the full story, go to KennyBarnwell.com.

9

The hope that doesn't disappoint: a journey through suffering

Jen's story

I've always been a feeler. A personality test once told me I was 98 per cent 'feeler,' and I've always felt *deeply*, for better and for worse. As one of four kids, born in Canada near the Rocky Mountains, I grew up with a sensitivity that allowed me to connect with the world around me in a profound way. But it also meant that when life was hard, I didn't just feel it, I was often overwhelmed by it.

There were seasons, especially in my younger years, where a quiet depression would settle over me. I'd be easily swept away by my emotions, and I didn't have the tools to fight back. I carried a gnawing sense of low self-worth, a feeling that I was an 'inconvenience', a burden on others, perhaps, or just not quite enough. It was a lie that whispered to me constantly, especially in a world that thrives on comparison and busyness.

But here's the truth that changed everything: if those thoughts were real, if my worth was truly so insignificant, then the gospel couldn't be true. The thought struck me with such force: Who would die for an inconvenience? Who would rise again for someone who believed it would be better if they weren't here? Jesus' sacrifice shows that I have immeasurable worth, and that started a quiet but powerful shift in my heart. Over time, I've been learning to fight back with that truth, especially when I feel exhausted, burnt out, and that battle in my mind intensifies.

My understanding of this journey was given a powerful framework by a verse I've come to hold dear. It's from Romans and it describes a kind of spiritual alchemy. A journey I never expected to produce suffering was the perfect storm to test this promise.

> Not only so, but we also glory in our sufferings,
> because we know that suffering produces perseverance;

> perseverance, character; and character, hope. And hope does not put us to shame, because God's love has been poured out into our hearts through the Holy Spirit, who has been given to us. Romans 5:3–5 (NIV)

Suffering that produced endurance

What started as a hopeful adventure to a new country became the most prolonged, significant period of suffering in my life. It was a battle for my hope, identity and mental well-being. From start to finish, my immigration process was 17 years. It was a bureaucratic nightmare filled with legal fees, endless paperwork, and the constant fear of rejection from even those closest to me. It was a fight for my dreams when all hope seemed to be lost.

This wasn't just a physical or logistical battle; it was a deeply spiritual and emotional one. The depression I had experienced before returned with a vengeance. There were days where getting out of bed felt impossible, my mind a relentless battleground of doubts: 'Are you sure you're meant to be here? Are you a fool for fighting so hard? Maybe you're just an inconvenience to this country, too.' My resilience was at zero, and I felt completely empty.

Yet, in that void, I clung to the promise of Romans 5. The suffering didn't break me, it forged an endurance I never knew I had. I learned to keep going even when I didn't see a way forward. It was a day-by-day, minute-by-minute choice to persevere. This wasn't about grit; it was about God's grace. He was with me in the trenches, a constant presence I could feel even when the world around me felt unstable. He provided in miraculous ways, often at the very last moment –11th-hour vibes for days!

I remember staring at an invoice from the most expensive and accomplished immigration lawyer in my city who had told me I had no pathway to permanent residency. Knowing I had nothing left to give, I cried out to God in desperation. That night I woke to the Holy Spirit telling me to 'look again' and I found a pathway myself that the number-one immigration lawyer didn't know about!

This specific year was one of constantly going back to God in my emptiness and telling him exactly what I needed and when. Each of these moments God was sustaining me, showing me that the suffering was not in vain, and that I could, and would, endure – and that He would provide exactly what I needed.

Endurance that produced character

The endurance I found wasn't just about staying the course; it was about a profound change within me. The constant struggle of the immigration process, and God's consistent faithfulness through it, began to refine my character. The impatience I used to feel was replaced with a deeper trust in God's timing. The anxiousness I battled was replaced with a steady sense of peace, even in the midst of uncertainty. The self-doubt I had always struggled with was being dismantled by a growing knowledge that I was seen, known and valued by God.

My identity was no longer rooted in my own strength or achievements, or in the validation of others. It became rooted in Christ. The struggle taught me to lean on Him completely, to acknowledge my own weakness so that His strength could be made perfect. This was the character being forged in the fire of my suffering, a character that was humble, resilient and utterly dependent on the love and grace of God.

This was the journey that led me to truly believe that my worth was not tied to my accomplishments or my circumstances, but to the unshakeable love of Jesus. He saw me in the trenches and was with me every step of the way.

Character that produced hope

The hope described in Romans isn't a wish; it's an anchor for the soul. The character forged during my years of immigration was the wellspring of this hope. My life became a testament to the promise that God is faithful, that He provides, and that He is intimately involved in the details of our lives.

My family is incredibly close, even though we are spread across four different time zones. I have a twin brother, a younger brother, and my parents. Our family is a constant source of love and support. But our fortress of hope was tested in a way I could never have imagined.

Just under two years ago, my beautiful sister passed away. She had fought a long battle with mental health and addiction. The grief of losing her to an overdose was immense, a new kind of suffering that felt all-consuming. The void she left behind was profound, but the hope that had been forged in me over the years held fast.

The character I had built through endurance became a foundation in the face of this unimaginable sorrow. I held onto the promise that God would never put us to shame. The hope I had was not a denial of the pain, but an unwavering belief that God was present in the messiest, most heartbreaking parts of our lives. I knew with every fibre of my being that Avy's battles did not define her worth in God's eyes, and that she was not an inconvenience to Him. This hope was my fortress. It's a hope that sustains my parents as they now care for Avy's three children. It's a hope that allows me to look forward, knowing that God's love is the one constant in a world of change and sorrow.

This hope does not disappoint. It is a hope that has been poured into our hearts through the Holy Spirit, enabling us to face the struggles of life and to find healing in God.

My message to anyone who is battling with self-worth or suffering through a difficult season is this: put on the mind of Christ. It's never too early and never too late to do the work of renewing your mind. Your thoughts shape your reality, and the enemy loves to lie to us about who we are. But when we align our thoughts with God's truth, everything changes. Your identity is secure in Christ. You are deeply loved, wanted and chosen.

10

Heard of or seen?

Debbie's story

> I had only heard about you before,
> but now I have seen you with my own eyes.
> Job 42:5 (NLT)

For many, the year 2008 will be remembered as the year of global recession; for me it was a new beginning, from thinking there had to be more to life than what I was living to realising there was a better future for me.

January 2008, I flew to Atlanta for a business training seminar in desperation for my little company to succeed. As that weekend progressed, I was recognising so many of the principles to generate income and grow in leadership were in the Bible. I had attended Church of England schools and we went to a local church as a family but our involvement was more about hopeful belief than true dedication.

I began to feel increasingly uncomfortable and started skipping a few sessions in preference for a glass of wine and cigarettes. Annoyingly though, the trainer's team were persistent in getting to know me. There seemed no polite way of escape.

> Before they call, I will answer; while they are yet
> speaking, I will hear. Isaiah 65:24 (NIV)

Returning home I was deeply troubled, and life was becoming even more unbearable. I would waver between ending my life or just walking away and living on the streets. The latter was an issue because even in that deep place of anguish and dread, I was concerned about not having money to have my hair done!

Peace, happiness and sleep eluded me. It was on one of these nights that, instead of getting up for yet another cigarette, I cried out a silent yet heartfelt, 'God, if you are real, if you are who the trainer Dani Johnson says you are, then you need to do something and do it *now!*' Surprisingly, I remember drifting effortlessly off to sleep.

Two days later, I received a phone call from Dani Johnson's office, asking me if I would organise her debut 'First Steps to Success' conference in the UK. Kerching!

I momentarily forgot about God. Instead, I was focused on this opportunity landing in my lap as it could turn my life around financially. God didn't stop there. He had radical, inconceivable plans. Not only did He throw me front and centre into this highly successful global company to organise this hugely sought-after event in London, but He brought who I now believe was an angel. She became involved in one of my businesses, through the *Guardian* newspaper, to partner with God's plans for my life. She never did any business but would call me each week and share engaging stories of life. I believe God was using this angel to prepare my heart for what was to come.

> You did not choose Me, but I chose you.
> John 15:16 (NIV)

Just prior to this event I was undergoing tests to finally establish a diagnosis for why I had been in so much pain, with increased abdominal swelling and so sick for many months. Scans revealed a complex cluster of cysts or tumours on my ovary which had erupted and were bleeding. Due to further symptoms, I had colonoscopies, biopsies and various tests to see if cancer had developed in my bowel and bladder, as the consultant suspected.

There was no logical reason why I would even attend the conference, as I was too sick and in so much pain, other than to ensure the event went well and that I would be in receipt of a handsome commission cheque. Plus, the angel in disguise was insisting I attend. God used so many others to make sure I was there, one way or another.

As the conference, got underway, on 14 June 2008, I became more unwell, barely making it through the day. I was dreading the evening session 'Spiritual Equipping' where the trainer Dani Johnson would speak directly from the Bible. There was no way out of it, but I had a plan! I gave my team the heads-up that I was going to sit at the back to make a quick exit as soon as I could, unnoticed.

However, I became aware of the sensation of being sort of stuck to my seat and some of the words were cutting deep. When I heard from the speaker, 'Many are called, few are chosen', there was an involuntary breaking of my heart vocalising 'God, choose me'. I had no idea what I asked for, the implications or consequences.

People were being called to the front – I'd never heard of altar calls, so again no idea of what was happening. I got up from my seat but instead of making a discreet exit, I was strangely drawn to the front, as if my body and will had been taken over.

I found myself at the front repeating words of a prayer, but I don't think I finished it because my voice and all those around me were becoming distant. I noticed I was hemmed in by a sea of people I didn't recognise, but they too faded away. Suddenly, I was drawn up into this light, the brightest, whitest light I had ever seen. It seemed to be coming from a window-like opening in the sky, yet I was in a conference ballroom! It was then I realised that the room no longer existed. Very difficult to articulate, the Apostle Paul says it best,

> For instance, I know a man who, fourteen years ago, was seized by Christ and swept in ecstasy to the heights of heaven. I really don't know if this took place in the body or out of it; only God knows.
>
> 2 Corinthians 12:2 (MSG)

As the light got brighter, I became distraught beyond words. Shame and disgust overwhelmed me. As I began weeping copiously, all I could see were globs of dirt falling off me. It was like my tears and the light were washing me clean. I heard myself saying 'I'm sorry', over and over again. As the last bit of dirt fell away, I heard a voice saying, 'Look up'.

Next to, but also part of the same window where the light was coming from, another opened. I am not sure whether I was raised up towards the figure coming towards me or the figure was descending, or a combination of both. All I know is that I found myself standing before a man dressed in layers of the coloured robes of a king; jewels sparkled, golden threads of His garments shone with such a brilliance.

He smiled at me like someone who knew me, genuinely loved me and was happy to be with me. As I looked into His eyes, I became overwhelmed, drowning in pools of indescribable intense love. His love kept flowing; even when I didn't think my body could take any more, there was no end. Even so, incredibly, my mind was still trying to reason with this, and I remember saying in my heart, my thoughts, 'Are you Jesus?'

The most glorious smile radiated from Him, and I heard the words 'I Am'. Next, I watched the hand of Jesus come towards me, the sleeve of His robes draped but barely touching me. As His hand rested on my head something happened to my body, like a powerful surge of electricity. My heart began to beat so hard and fast, I could hardly breathe, and I thought I must be dying. I then found myself falling; even though I hit the ground, I rebounded on the most beautiful soft down of feathers that cupped and cradled my body.

I recall being hoisted up onto the platform, but before anyone came near me, I fell under the weight of His glory and lay frozen like a statue for what seemed to be hours before I was eventually carried away.

Unbeknown to me at the time, the room erupted. People were falling under the power of God around me and demons were fleeing out everywhere. Well-known ministers who happened to be there, came to help the speaker bring control back to the room and help those affected by the presence of God and set free.

> Where the Spirit of the Lord is, there is freedom.
> 2 Corinthians 3:17 (NIV)
> Don't forget to show hospitality to strangers, for in doing so, some have entertained angels without knowing it. Hebrews 13:2 (NLT)

In the middle of the night, I was woken up with the word 'Seek'. I sensed I needed to write something down. So, I picked up my cigarettes and keys and went in search of paper and pen so as not to disturb my roommates. As I approached the front desk a lovely man dressed as a concierge came to me asking if I would I like a pen and paper. As he brought them to me, he led me to an outside table to sit at and he offered to bring me a hot chocolate. I noticed he remained watchful but at a bit of a distance.

Suddenly I found myself writing, 'Ask, and it will be given to you; seek, and you will find; knock, and it will be opened to you.' I was later told these words were from Matthew 7:7 and they remain etched on my heart today.

Another person on the trainer's team ventured to tell me I had been baptised and filled with the Holy Spirit, to which I replied in terror, *'What is that?'* I had no clue what was happening to me; everything seemed so strange and detached from life as I knew it. Even going out on the street, colours of trees, flowers, the sky were all so vibrant, so intense that it made me feel woozy, as though drunk. I could also see into people's minds. Their emotions in particular were transparent. When I saw someone sad or hurting, I felt their sorrow, their pain so deeply.

> Praise the Lord, my soul, and forget not all his benefits,
> who forgives all your sins and heals all your diseases.
> Psalm 103:2–3 (NIV)

On my return home I went back to the hospital for follow-up scans and test results. The consultant was frustrated and declared that the scan machine must be faulty, so we had to wait for another to become available.

Not satisfied with the readings, I had to undergo another more invasive scan on my ovary. The doctor posted up on the wall two images. One showing the severity of the diseased ovary and then one that showed a perfectly healthy ovary. The medical staff were perplexed, because they said even if the body had healed itself, there would have been scar tissue as evidence of what had been, but there was none!

Next stop – the surgeon who performed the colonoscopy. He sat me down and said 'I do not understand this. I was convinced I removed diseased tissue.' He then put a sheet of paper in my hand with a list, telling me that normally they say if you have five of these symptoms, see your doctor. 'I am telling you, if you have one of these symptoms, you call me directly. Here, take my card.'

We used to have a family history of ovarian and uterine cancer; in fact my mother passed a few years prior from cancer. So not only did God heal me, but I also believe that night a curse was broken off my family.

> Being confident of this very thing, that He who
> has begun a good work in you will carry it on to
> completion until the day of Jesus Christ.
> Philippians 1:6 (NIV)

I had been smoking since the age of 16 and very heavily since my late teens. For more than 30 years I had been smoking an average of two packs a day. As I became increasingly and deeply immersed into this incredible relationship with the Holy Spirit, I was getting distressed as I continued to smoke, yet Jesus had saved my life only weeks before.

Over the years, I had tried everything available to help me give up smoking: patches, group therapy, counselling, hypnotherapy; doctors even put me on Prozac more than once. My nicotine craving was so bad I would wake up most nights in the early hours to have at least one cigarette. Once the smoking ban came in… it was torture. As soon as I arrived anywhere, I would search out the smoking areas. Flights were a nightmare. Long-haul disastrous; the lengths I would go to, to get through was desperately sad. I would spend a fortune on patches, gum or any substitute that was legal. I was so trapped by the addiction, miserable and scared. So, I said to Jesus, 'You are the only one who can help me quit.' I didn't set a date or occasion as I had on previous attempts but left it up to Him!

I planned to attend another conference in Atlanta run by the same Christian trainer, Dani Johnson, and put myself on the list to be baptised.

The night of 4th December 2008 I was baptised in a hotel pool. Again, the beautiful, heavy, *Kavod*, glory of God fell on me. I remained passed out in the water for some time; my body being literally cradled by Simon, an Australian minister who sacrificed his rather expensive suit to be in the water with me!

When I eventually came out of the pool, I had no desire for a cigarette and I have not smoked since.

> Be alert and of sober mind. Your enemy the devil prowls around like a roaring lion looking for someone to devour. 1 Peter 5:8 (NIV)

Three days later I was woken with a jeering, mocking voice saying, 'Isn't it time you had a cigarette?' I had been so completely delivered that I had forgotten I had ever smoked and for three days I'd been carrying round a pack of cigarettes in the front pouch of my handbag. Plus, there were 400 in my suitcase to take home.

Every now and again the enemy would come back at me to tempt me: 'If God delivered you from smoking, you could have one…it won't make you addicted again. You could just be a social smoker.' All sorts of tricks the enemy would use, but the Lord helped me even more by creating in me such a hunger for Him that I craved Jesus and His word instead of craving a cigarette.

Has my life been without its challenges? No. Jesus says to us:

> In Me you may have peace. In this world you will have trouble. But take heart, I have overcome the world.
> John 16:33 (NIV)

I know I am loved. I am not alone in any situation. The Lord is my protector, my provider, my healer, my helper, my friend. I pray that whoever reads this testimony of God's goodness will have ears to hear and open the door to Jesus.

> Behold, I stand at the door and knock. If anyone hears My voice and opens the door, I will come in to him and dine with him, and he with Me.
> Revelation 3:20 (NIV)

11

After all these years

Nuno's story

In 2019, I moved to the United Kingdom (UK) after receiving a series of dreams and visions from the Lord. I moved out of my comfort zone – family, friends, church, work, and South Africa – surrendered my questions, dealt with my fears and insecurities, and moved in obedience to Him, and the Lord supernaturally provided about £30,000 in the most unusual way.

Before I moved to the UK, the Lord told me that I would grow tremendously in my prophetic gifting in my season in the UK, which I struggled to believe as my mind could not comprehend how I could possibly grow more by living in a more secular country. I spent time in prayer asking God for divine appointments with the people I needed to connect with.

I asked Him to plant me in a church that looked like the early church described in the book of Acts, as at the time I was reading Acts. I felt the global church did not fully look like the early church, but had instead become more institutionalised and religious. On my first Sunday in the UK, I arrived at a small church, and the lady who welcomed me at the door, prompted by the Holy Spirit, at once introduced me to a couple who had done ministry in South Africa and Mozambique. I was immediately welcomed with love and warmth by Ed and Pamela.

Our hearts instantly connected, and they anointed my feet, prayed for me, and welcomed me to the UK in the physical sense and in the spirit. After church, they took me out for my first full-English breakfast in the UK, and we shared life together over a meal. On my second Sunday, Ed and Pamela introduced me to a ministry where I eventually got planted, trained and mentored by seasoned global prophets for two years, who continue to pour into my life.

The Lord gave me genuine and authentic community within five days of arriving in this country, and through Ed and Pamela, my community increased. I have never met such selfless people, who loved a stranger (me) unconditionally, instantly after meeting me and gave of their possessions and time to be a blessing to me. The Lord truly honoured my prayers and gave me a church and a community that resembled the early church described in the book of Acts.

> All the believers were united in heart and mind. And they felt that what they owned was not their own, so they shared everything they had. Acts 4:32–35 (NLT).

God completely blew me away with His love, goodness, provision and favour in my time in the UK. This leap of faith taught me, as a man who at times wants to be in control and know every step of the journey ahead, that surrendering to the Lord and trusting Him unconditionally in the unknown is one important way to experience His provision and breakthrough.

I absolutely loved my season in the UK, and I never wanted it to end. However, the Lord started closing doors when I tried prolonging my stay and He started speaking to me through dreams and visions about returning to South Africa. I initially did not want to return to South Africa, and I resisted the Lord and couldn't comprehend why He would want to remove me from the country where I had had the best church experience and so much more. The UK, my church and my friends had become my comfort zone, and I had to lay it all down in obedience to the Lord and return to South Africa. My leaders blessed and released me, and I flew back to South Africa.

During my first night in Johannesburg, I had a prophetic dream where the Lord spoke to me about what He would do in and through me and He told me He would raise me to become a leader. I really struggled with the season of transition back to South Africa. My heart and mind were not in South Africa – all I wanted was to return to the UK, my church and friends. I applied for a few jobs in the UK while in South Africa and got rejected.

I struggled to adapt to living in two cities within a year and making new friends post-Covid as some of my old friends had either moved to new locations or into new relational seasons. I also struggled to find a new church as I kept getting caught up in comparing any new church I visited to my church in the UK.

Starting afresh is never easy, but I learnt to surrender my former season, the transition and my questions to the Lord so that I could receive the fullness of what He had in store for me in my new season, and I sought Him for wisdom and direction. He was faithful to give me a new community locally and internationally, and challenged my quest to find the perfect church as there is no perfect church. However, He taught me the importance of being planted in a local church, fellowshipping with believers and being a gift and servant to the body of Christ.

In 2021, I had a dream where the Lord showed me the company I would work for, and three months later, I got a job at the very same company. I took up a leadership position just as He had shown me in the dream I had on my first night back in South Africa. The Lord gave me favour with my clients, colleagues, and godly wisdom and knowledge to execute my work with excellence, and I progressed rapidly within the organisation, eventually managing a business unit and a team of nineteen employees based in Sub-Saharan Africa and Europe.

In 2024 a lady I managed, falsely accused me and sowed lies about my character and leadership in my work environment. My manager and the human resources officer believed her one-sided false narrative as they had a friendship and had worked together at another company. I felt rejected and betrayed by a manager I trusted, and I felt rejected by God and couldn't comprehend why He would allow me to go through such challenging circumstances. I felt like quitting my job and even applied for other jobs. I experienced a lot of emotional distress, lost my motivation to work, questioned my identity and whether I was even called to leadership.

It was challenging to have to continue going to work with the same people who accused me, and even more challenging to have to lead a large international team knowing my heart was wounded, and that as a leader I was not fully present or engaged mentally, emotionally and physically with my work and team. I navigated this difficult time by literally crying out to God for help, wisdom and strategy on how to navigate the season. He was faithful, and He loved, comforted and guided me through, and promised to do justice.

Reading my Bible and engaging in praise and worship helped me to keep my eyes on Jesus, His truth and not on the storms of life, which gave me clarity and vision during this time. Praying for and blessing my enemies several times helped me to let go of the offence and bitterness in my heart and to receive emotional healing from the Lord. Sharing my challenges openly with friends I do life with helped me not to be in isolation, but to be in a loving and wise community that also challenged the lies I had unconsciously partnered with and the victim mentality I had embraced.

In the final meeting I had with my accuser and the human resources officer, the Lord gave me favour and wisdom, and I was able to dismantle the lies and false accusations that had been sown against me with truth and evidence. Over the next couple of months after this meeting, the Lord reversed the reputational damage that had occurred, and my leadership was publicly endorsed. I ended up being the only leader from my department to be recognised for excellence in leadership, and my enemies had to witness the mighty and faithful hand of the Lord upon my life.

The most important lesson I learnt in this season is that tribulation is not a setback, but a divine set-up that will lead to promotion. Being a leader in the corporate world for a multinational organisation is not as glamorous as people portray it to be on social media. It's a difficult environment where most people wear masks to hide their brokenness and where many people lose themselves and pursue the idols of the world – such as wealth and fame.

I personally have had moments where I felt like giving up because it was too much and too hard for me to bear. It is a great honour to be entrusted with leadership by the Lord, to serve people, and formulate strategies that impact the lives of people globally, but what people don't see are the sacrifices you need to make; the discipline you need to adopt to remain focused, passionate, intentional, relevant and grounded; the competition, backstabbing and false accusations you often need to deal with; how challenging it is to submit to unrighteous leaders and to challenge their unrighteous decisions; and how you need to continue to work on yourself as an individual and a leader, spiritually, mentally, emotionally and physically.

During a turbulent 2024, the Lord instructed me to buy a property in Johannesburg and to pay off the loan within a year, which was a word I struggled to believe as the interest rates were high, and I did not have enough money saved up. However, confirmation came through a prophetic word from a dear friend of mine in the United States of America, Rebecca, who indicated where I lived was going to change as the Lord was repositioning me. I received her prophetic word literally a few hours after viewing a property and I instantly knew I had to take this step of faith.

Before I purchased the property, by the grace of God and to my surprise, my salary increased three times within a year. I managed to secure a good interest rate with my bank, and I eventually bought the property the Lord showed me. My interest rate was lowered three times after I purchased my property and I also received a couple of refunds from my bank and vouchers from my employer, which helped me to purchase appliances for my kitchen and bedding for one of the bedrooms. The Lord gave me financial wisdom, favour and provision, which enabled me to pay off the property loan fully within a year.

My journey with the Lord over the last five years has been both beautiful and messy. I encountered Him in new ways and experienced His love, mercy, grace, forgiveness, kindness, patience, healing, faithfulness, provision and relentless pursuit of me. I've grown in intimacy with Him and in my spiritual gifts and today have more wisdom and a greater knowledge of my calling on Earth. I have also gone through painful and difficult seasons which I initially struggled to understand and navigate as they tested my faith and exposed my brokenness.

However, the Lord used these seasons to heal me and to grow me more into the image of Christ when I surrendered to Him and held onto His faithfulness and goodness, even when I had a hard time believing and seeing it. The Father knows both sorrow and joy, and He is always with us through every season and longs for us to lean into the love, healing, security and provision we can only find in Him.

> The LORD is close to the broken-hearted; he rescues those whose spirits are crushed. Psalm 34:18 (NLT).

After all these years, I can boldly and wholeheartedly proclaim that the God my grandparents loved, the God my parents walk with and the God I love and serve even today, has never changed and He never will. He is the same yesterday, today and forever. His love, goodness and faithfulness are unwavering and His pursuit of me is relentless. No force on Earth or beyond can ever separate me from His love. This is the legacy I carry. This is the hope I live by. This is the story I leave with you.

> I will instruct you and teach you in the way you should go; I will counsel you with My loving eye on you.
> Psalm 32:8 (NIV).

12

No house. No job. No backup plan. Just God

Donna's story

I saw the phone number flash on my ringing phone. Answering it I blurted out, 'I know why you're calling, so how much time do we have?' The Lord had forewarned our family that this phone call was coming so I wasn't surprised and yet I was still disappointed that it had finally come.

It was our real-estate company. We had rented the house we were living in for over 18 years and we now had six children, five cars, with one of our sons owning and operating an online board game business with 157 boxes of inventory that we were stocking to help support him.

The real-estate owner called as he thought we would prefer a call rather than a letter. He told us we had three months to move out. The housing market had taken a real hit and rental properties were few and far between. My husband had also lost his job and my struggling business was not covering the bills. I had never failed to pay a bill in my life before, so this was a painfully difficult and somewhat humbling time for me.

The house we lived in was two storeys and the main bathroom on the top floor had been leaking through the ceiling below on and off for over ten years. Previous attempts to fix it had failed and I felt the Lord saying that the owner would ask us to leave so that he could gut the bathroom and renovate the house, and increase the rent – and that's exactly what happened. The house was brand new when we moved in (another God story) so renovations were desperately needed.

I told my family the news, and none of them were surprised as God had prepared them too, then I went to my laptop to begin looking for homes. The familiar and kind voice of the Lord spoke to me in my mind, 'What are you doing?' I simply answered with, 'We need to move out, just as you said, so I need to start looking for somewhere to live.' God had other ideas. 'No, I don't want you looking until two months have passed.'

'You've got to be kidding me!' I gasped. Oh great. Another test. I told my husband what I believed the Lord had said, and asked him to seek the Lord for confirmation. It came in many ways.

OK. We're on another teaching moment and learning curve with the Lord. Buckle up!

> Dear brothers and sisters, when troubles of any kind come your way, consider it an opportunity for great joy. For you know that when your faith is tested, your endurance has a chance to grow. So let it grow, for when your endurance is fully developed, you will be perfect and complete, needing nothing.
> James 1:2–4 (NLT)

During this time, I learnt a little of what these verses mean. When you're in a time of testing, you get to know Father God in ways that you wouldn't in other circumstances, and this brings you joy. When you begin to understand just how committed He is to you and that nothing takes Him by surprise, your whole life changes.

Having six children, I learnt very quickly that not everyone understands your own journey of obedience with the Lord, so you need to be very particular in who you share your journey with. I learnt only to share what was going on with those who had faith for the impossible, who would speak life into us and our situation, and those who would pray as the Lord led them, not out of their own thinking and opinion.

Hence, not many people knew our predicament. We would serve at church on a Sunday and throughout the week, homeschool our youngest children, run to and from work and activities with those who didn't have a car, and I would run our business – all without people knowing.

Now, was I stressed? I wish I could say no but I was still in the process of learning how to live in supernatural peace. I was having heart palpitations, my hair was falling out, I was hardly sleeping, and I consistently had adrenaline rushing around my body which meant I was on high alert 24/7. Not a healthy way to live.

So, there we were. Everything in our home is packed, we're living out of boxes, and we're not able to look at houses to rent. I admit, a couple of times during those first two months I opened my laptop and began browsing. To say it was awful was an understatement and extremely discouraging. I looked at five and six-bedroom homes and the rental prices were over the top. The photos were taken in a way that makes the rooms look much bigger than they actually are.

God again would interrupt me with, 'What are you doing?' I told Him, in no uncertain terms, to go away and if He wasn't going to help me, to stop talking to me. I was just being honest. I know that's shocking yet here's what I want you to know: Father God knows what you're feeling and thinking anyway, and He much prefers it when you're completely honest with Him instead of saying what you think He wants to hear. You have permission to do so.

I have relational equity with the Lord. I have always been honest with Him and He appreciates it because that's what friends do. However, I also understand that He is God and I submit to His instruction because I know that He knows best. After I have my rant, I ask Him for His perspective and to help me to align mine with His.

OK, so I stopped looking. The weeks went by and with exactly one month to go, we began seriously looking for a new home. I wasn't prepared for what I discovered. Five-bedroom homes mean four tiny bedrooms and a study with no door for a fifth 'bedroom'. None of our living room furniture would have fitted in these spaces and our industrial washing machine wouldn't fit into any of the laundries. We saw houses with no doors on the bathrooms, living areas that were in no way conducive to family relationships, garages that wouldn't fit any of our cars, and streets that were so narrow there was no room to park in them anyway.

It was very discouraging and all I could do was say, 'God always has a solution' while holding back tears that threatened to overflow at any moment. The prospect of us being homeless was crushing and it was worse still because, in my mind, I wasn't making enough money to support the family. I felt I was failing in more ways than one.

The day before our eviction date I called the real-estate owner and told him of our predicament. He suggested that our kids move out because if he had an application for a family of eight come across his desk, he wouldn't even look at it. Okay then.

The eviction date had passed and we shifted to looking at four-bedroom homes. They were worse! How could this be? Doesn't God tell us to walk with integrity and obey the laws of the land? Wasn't He meant to be our helper in time of need? Where was He and what was He doing? I didn't understand.

It was two weeks later when we eventually found a house that was on 5.2 acres of land, shared with another house. I knew immediately this was the place for us. It had been vacant for over 12 months as the landlord didn't like any of the previous applications presented to them. Regardless, we applied.

While waiting to hear about our application, we kept looking for a house. One week later, the owner's agent called asking for more information. They were shocked that our application was the first that the owners were interested in. I sent the information and for another week... nothing.

Our original real-estate company rang and I ignored the call. I rang the new agents to ask them for an update. They didn't know and said they'd get back to me. Waiting for their answer was excruciating. But soon after, they called back. I held the phone to my belly and yelled, 'We have the house!', so my husband and children could hear me downstairs. I think the whole neighbourhood heard me. I cried as I was thanking the lady on the other end of the phone. The tears flowed along with the gut-wrenching sobs of relief. Thank you, Father God!

One month and one day after our eviction date, we moved house... and we absolutely love it. Regarding the house, I had asked the Lord for bay windows, no carpet, a walk-in pantry, a walk-in wardrobe, a covered veranda out the back so we could sit outside even in the rain, ducted air conditioning and a large double garage with a wide and long driveway so that all of our cars would fit. Most of these features we've never had before and God granted them all!

Lessons learnt

God is not at all concerned about our time constraints. I can look at this experience and say that He was late. In an earthly sense, He was, yet He was right on time from His perspective. I cannot put my own expectations onto God and tell Him how to do anything. He sees the whole picture and I don't.

I learnt how to use God's strength and not my own. When you're stressed, exhausted and can't see a way forward, you take the next step and God's strength then fills you. His strength doesn't come before you need it. Suddenly, you realise that you're more resilient and stronger than you ever thought possible because you're walking with His power helping you, every step of the way.

I need to think about God instead of thinking about myself. Do I choose to hold onto the truth that God always has a solution and He's always working behind the scenes, or do I look at my confusing surroundings and believe that this is all there is? I could spend my days focusing on my lack and the situation around me or I could focus on the fact that God never changes, He's so good and that He knows what He's doing. He only has the best outcomes for you and me, every time.

Every moment is made up of my own choices. The stress was unbelievable and every moment I needed to make a choice: do I keep going, putting one foot in front of the other, or do I collapse in a heap and give up? One of the most powerful gifts that we were ever given is our power of choice. Every day you have the power to choose what you think about and what you focus on.

Philippians 4:8 gives us the blueprint of exactly what to do:

> And now, dear brothers and sisters, one final thing. Fix your thoughts on what is true, and honourable, and right, and pure, and lovely, and admirable. Think about things that are excellent and worthy of praise. (NLT)

At the time of writing, we have been in this house for just over one year and every day is a celebration of what God did for our family. We absolutely love living here and the lessons learnt about the Lord are invaluable and can't be learned in any other way except through trial, testing and His provision.

++++++++++++++

Discover a vibrant sisterhood where Kingdom-minded women step into boldness, clarity and being led by Holy Spirit every day. If you're ready to grow in hearing God's voice, in activating your prophetic gifts, receiving strategy and walking confidently in your purpose, without the pressure to have it all figured out, the 'Women Boldly Living Holy Spirit Led Community' is for you.

www.courageouskingdomwomen.com/lhsl-community

13

Found

Joan's story

Have you ever been in the wilderness, and been lost? You can hear your name being called yet you cannot tell which direction the voice is coming from? That was me. I was fourteen and the teachers were asking us students what we want to be when we grow up.

That age is a crucial time in the life of any youth. So many changes to deal with. I was not an avid student. I was told to sit still and put in the 'special' class. Of all the activities in my young life, school was my least favourite. I was a mover. To sleep at night I rocked in bed, hummed, kicked my leg and sucked my thumb (until I was 12), all that just to get to sleep.

In school, I had to sit still. When I did this, it was like my ears fell off. I could see the lips of the teacher moving but nothing was heard. School was like being lost in a wilderness. Now in junior high, they wanted us to determine what we wanted to be when all this education was said and done.

I remember thinking 'I don't even know why I am here on this planet, never mind what I want to be. What is the point? The purpose to being alive anyway?'

My grandparents prayed so I surmised they must know God, and God must know the answer. However, they lived in another city, and we were on the farm. As a youngster I had made deals with 'God'. 'God if you help me out, I promise to be good and obey my parents.' Things would work out, but I reneged on my promise. There was literally no internal fortitude to follow through and obey them. I knew lying was unacceptable, but my lies were, just let's say, 'the truth with a slight bend to make me look innocent'.

I did crave feeling clean inside, but no number of hot baths seemed to go deep enough, to reach the dark places my mind went to. I had moments when I was intentionally mean and hurtful to those weaker, smaller or younger. I would regret my behaviour, it made me feel ugly and cruel. I hated this feeling but how to get free of it? This feeling took root in my heart leading to me being debilitated by a lack of self-respect. Like pulling the plug on a full sink of water, a vortex was created that pulled everything down.

I rode the school bus with a neighbour who went to church with her family in the town a few miles away. I thought that is where you would find God, though I knew details of her life and didn't see any real differences between our struggles of youth.

Her family picked me up in a motorhome and we drove to church. I wasn't familiar with the rituals and seemed to be out of sync but followed the motions anyway. I had no understanding of the classes set aside for us. The terminology and ideas were like a foreign language. And the room was so very small for us we had to sit squeezed together on the steps. I was not permitted to participate in walking up to the front and getting the wafer put in my mouth by the leader. In the end, I still did not know why I was on the planet; I could see no clear purpose, nor the steps on how to find God.

When my grandparents would visit, I had great excitement. Grandma brought cookies or slippers she made. As kids we were expected to go play and let them visit. I wanted to be close to them. When they were around for a meal, we would listen as Grandpa would bless the food. He would bow and pray long prayers giving thanks for so many things I had never thought to be thankful for. Grandma and Grandpa were invariably happy and appeared always to have money, as they would give us children two dollars each. Grandma and Grandpa were the closest thing I knew to how God must be.

Saturday was 'clean your room day'. I think it was really 'Mom needs time for herself day'. My sister and I had our own rooms in the basement. She was at a friend's one particular Saturday, and I was sorting through my treasures in the bottom drawer of the dresser. I found a small bright blue book I had received in Grade three when the Gideons* visited our school and gave one to each student. By now I could read and was curious what the book was about.

I randomly opened it and began to read. I do not know how long I read, before I closed the book and got on my knees and began to say, 'forgive me, forgive me, forgive me.' I prayed this phrase over and over again. (The church I had been to with my neighbour had prayers that you were supposed to repeat.) Not knowing how many times to say this, I felt I had said it long enough to cover all the dark and nasty things I had been part of or done. I sensed my room was brighter than before and somehow though I was known as 'Boney Joanie' because I was so thin, I somehow felt lighter as if I had shed some weight. I went upstairs and found a cracker and a glass of juice and took them downstairs to my room and got back on my knees. I had no insight or understanding of the significance of these things, only that you had to be someone special to eat them.

In that moment I felt warm and significant, though I could not explain why. That moment something in me changed. I felt clean, new, full of light in the places that were so dark before. The kids on the school bus and at the school noticed. My foul mouth was purged. I was kind. My teachers noticed. The greatest change of all was that the need or compulsion to constantly argue, challenge, be rude or disobey my parents had lost its power. I now felt like there was an energy inside that wanted to please them. I had wanted to before, yet now it was genuine. Not just to get my way but to bring them a gift of goodness, so to speak. This provoked them to revisit the church they knew in their courtship days.

It was only the beginning. Within months, they began attending a church and they took me to a house meeting. There was a relative there who I asked to speak with privately. We stepped away to another room and I explained how the good I wanted to do I couldn't, and the bad I didn't want to do I did. I wanted to know what changed in me. Was this real. Was this normal? She shared about the apostle Paul, who word for word explained the same struggle and how in my reading and prayer I had surrendered to God and become born again. Made new! Yes, it was real, and it was only the first step. She went on to pray with me the 'sinners' prayer' to confirm to me that it was now witnessed by another and now I was considered part of the family of God.

I was so excited. In the months that followed that day I could not stop reading my blue book. It was the New Testament. I was also given a whole Bible, both old and new testaments, and was in awe of how we came to be, in the book of Genesis. I had such a desire to tell everyone what had happened. How God found me. I had been lost, my heart was yearning and longing to know 'Why am I on the planet, why am I alive?' I look back and see how I could hear Him calling my insides to be different, clean, true, full of light. He knew I was searching for Him, so He kept calling my name. I remember that day, sitting on the floor by my bed with my back leaning against the bedframe, being in wonder at how I felt so clean and full of light and significant. Loved by God himself.

I still sit and think on these things. Now I know Him. The name of His Son, Jesus. My heart now is home to His Holy Spirit. The adventures, encounters and transformation, since being found by God, are so rich and beyond what this temporal existence can provide. I stay tuned to hearing and following the sound of His voice, knowing that even if I get lost, He calls my name, and I respond.

In being found, I have discovered my reason for existing. To know the One who knows me, who designed, created and made me unique (even the perpetual motion of my body is by design). I am the only me on the planet. *Yay!* He knew me, in heaven, before He breathed me into my mother's womb, before the darkness reigned in my heart and mind. He never lost sight of the original design he had for me. To this day He still calls me: significant, precious, an original, *beloved*. In responding with my heart and soul, I was found. Dear reader He is calling you too:

> I have other sheep that are not of this sheep pen. I must bring them also. They too will listen to my voice.
> John 10:16 (NIV)

> In the same way your Father in heaven is not willing that one of these little ones should perish.
> Matthew 18:14 (NIV)

I have since learned that 'Bible' stands for Basic Instructions Before Leaving Earth. I am so grateful I was given a Bible.

*Gideons: An organisation that printed and distributed Bibles in schools in the 1970s.
Thank you, Jesus.

14

When God came running

Marty's story

'Raaahhh!' came the primal scream ripping from my chest, raw and uncontainable, like the cry of a wounded wild animal. A wild animal trapped in complete despair and hopelessness. A moment in time when my existence on this planet felt totally devoid of meaning and purpose as I found myself imprisoned in a dungeon of abuse and control.

I would love to tell you that it was in that moment that Jesus revealed His love to me and I was born again! I would love to testify how I had reached rock bottom trying to navigate a life without Jesus in control and that, out of that moment of pure despair, I repented, and my life changed forever.

Sadly, I cannot. You see, I was a pastor and had been living for Jesus for decades! I had 'walked the talk' for 28 years as a born-again believer. I had given up everything in my home country, leaving my family and friends behind, moving to Germany to plant a church with my husband, taking our little boys of just one and two years old away from their grandparents, aunties and uncles. On the outside, my life looked full of adventure, as it should as one who had made the big sacrifices to follow the call.

My husband and I have always had a strong and beautiful marriage rooted in our friendship of many years, so that wasn't the problem. Our boys were healthy, happy and full of life pursuing their passions, so that wasn't the problem. The church we had planted 10 years previously was growing and thriving where God's precious Holy Spirit was welcome and active, so that wasn't the problem. My husband was a full-time pastor, and I was working full-time as a secretary for a law firm and our finances were healthy, so that wasn't the problem. On paper, everything was perfect!

However, in the background, the dark shadows of fear, control and punishment were never too far away. I could hide from them for a while, but they cast their darkness over me on a regular basis, and now, I just couldn't carry on any more.

You see, I'm a child of the so-called heavy shepherding movement of the 1970s. This was a time where there was excessive control from the church leadership. This meant I couldn't apply for a job without their input. I couldn't go to university as they needed my help in the church. It was blind obedience, and I thought this was normal.

I became a Christian in 1987 at the age of 18. Before my ultimate surrender to Jesus, I was a pure rebel, constantly in trouble with the authorities, in all forms. I won't go into the ins and outs of what that looked like but it wasn't pretty. Suffice to say, when I met Jesus, it was at a time when I was in a lot of trouble and very desperate.

The church I found myself in was loving, but strict and in all fairness, boundaries and disciplines were needed in my life and probably saved it many times. In my gratitude and desperate desire to be 'a good girl', I would hang on to every word the pastor said. I believed that he was the closest thing to God I had ever seen. If the pastor said black was white, then I would agree because, of course, he would be right and who am I to disagree or say any different?

Although this may have endeared me to the leaders of the churches I later joined, due to relocation, getting married, and so on, it was a problem...and a big problem. I ultimately found myself in a church network that looked wonderful on the outside. And if you toed the line, everything was fantastic and went smoothly.

Although there were several little red flags that concerned me over the years, about what I perceived to be a lack of grace or love in the church, the unhealthy striving for financial or numerical success, or maybe the odd 'white lie' told by the senior pastor to embellish a sermon point, I obeyed without question – which is what I was brought up spiritually to do, even if it went against my peace.

I closed my eyes to these little red flags for decades. After all, they were relatively minor but, as I got closer to the inner circle, I became acutely aware of the church politics fuelled by a culture of fear, punishment and reward. If you did and said what the senior leader liked, you were accepted into the inner circle. If you disagreed or disobeyed, you were accused of rebellion, even of witchcraft or having lost your way, and kicked out of the inner circle, cut off from everyone and everything you had ever known since being a part of the community.

And the saddest part? I thought this was normal and that God was the same! But now, here I was, thrown out of the inner circle for daring to raise an issue that I considered unrighteous and detrimental to the church at large. And that's when it started in earnest ... the abuse, the lies, the isolation and threats. I had poked the bear, and boy was he angry and ready to tear me to shreds.

I was shocked and horrified at the level of vengeance and curses that came my way for daring to disagree. Yet, this ministry network was all I had ever known! I had no one to turn to, no one to hear me, as I was told no one would believe the threats made against me, especially as the aggressor was a then-respected church leader in the city and country.

It was during this soul-destroying time that I cried out to heaven. 'Jesus, you said you came to set me free, but I feel more in chains now than I ever did!' As I read Danny Silk's book *The Culture of Honour*, my eyes were opened to a whole different Christianity.

I felt in chains because I had been led to believe that my protection from evil was found under the covering of this one particular expression of church and the man who led it. Should I ever leave, I would be leaving the covering and be opened up to all kinds of curses. I would be guilty of breaking covenant and therefore have no place left to serve God in His kingdom because I was untrustworthy. Covenant meant obedience and loyalty at all costs... even if it went against your peace or understanding.

But God...

> In my distress I called to the LORD;
>   I cried to my God for help.
> From His temple He heard my voice;
>   My cry came before Him, into His ears.
> The earth trembled and quaked,
>   And the foundations of the mountains shook;
>   They trembled because He was angry.
> Smoke rose from His nostrils;
>   Consuming fire came from His mouth,

Burning coals blazed out of it.
He parted the heavens and came down;
Dark clouds were under His feet.
He mounted the cherubim and flew;
He soared on the wings of the wind.
He made darkness His covering,
His canopy around Him –
The dark rain clouds of the sky.
Out of the brightness of His presence clouds advanced,
With hailstones and bolts of lightning.
The LORD thundered from heaven;
The voice of the Most High resounded.
He shot His arrows and scattered the enemy,
With great bolts of lightning He routed them.
The valleys of the sea were exposed
And the foundations of the earth laid
bare at your rebuke, LORD,
At the blast of breath from your nostrils.
He reached down from on high and took hold of me;
He drew me out of deep waters.
...He brought me out into a spacious place;
He rescued me because He delighted in me.
Psalm 18:6–16, 19 (NIV)

In that moment of complete despair, I experienced a side of our wonderful heavenly Father that I had never experienced before. I don't think I could word it any better than David in the Psalm above. As I cried out in desperation, many coincidences and divine appointments started happening that led me to an overwhelming revelation of the Father-heart of God. It was as if He swooped down and picked me up out of the fire.

I was reminded of when, as a little girl, some teenage boys had jumped on my little wooden dinghy (my dad owned a boat and the dinghy was how we got to shore when out on our travels), and I was distraught. I will never forget how my dad heard my cries and came running at the speed of an athlete to find out what was wrong and, goodness, when those boys saw him, they were very scared indeed. My dad heard the cry of distress and swooped down to save me.

Of course, the outworking of how our wonderful heavenly

Father swooped down to save me was a lot more intense and it would take me a whole book to describe in detail every promise, coincidence, God-ordained divine appointment and answered prayer that led to my ultimate freedom and release, two years later, from the church network that had caused me such distress. Those two years were walked out with a completely new perspective, genuinely knowing that God was for me, He wasn't angry and I wasn't going to be cursed for leaving that particular expression of the family of God. I wasn't forfeiting my destiny in order to obtain freedom from the control and abusive behaviour I had encountered. In fact, I truly was being taken to a spacious place. A place of grace and freedom.

This all happened between 2016 and 2018. Such a small blip in a lifetime, yet it marked me. Just like Jacob had been marked by God after wrestling all night with an angel, so I had been permanently marked during my journey into freedom. Our wonderful Father wastes nothing and since that time, my life's mission has been to bring others into the freedom and revelation of the true Father-heart of God. There is nothing that could ever cause me to doubt His love for me now. His goodness is ingrained deeply into every fibre of my being.

I am convinced that there is a fresh move of God happening where He is bringing His children back into healthy relationship with Him. Everywhere I go, I hear people talking about how they have encountered the Father-heart of God in a new way that has transformed their relationship with Him.

For years I saw God more like my boss and me a lowly employee who had to walk on eggshells in order to curry favour and keep in His good books, but God's heart is for us is to know Him as He truly is, our Father!

Maybe you are reading this and you are unsure if you see God through the lens of a boss or a Father. Let's invite Holy Spirit into the conversation as we look at the traits of both. These are not exhaustive, but will get you started on your journey of discovery.

Seeing God as boss

Transactional interactions: We see our relationship with God as a series of transactions where we perform duties to receive blessings or avoid punishment. Sounds harsh, but how many of us have been in need, let's say financial, and felt we couldn't believe God for His provision because we hadn't read the Bible enough that week?

Performance-based acceptance: Believing that God's love and acceptance depend on our achievements and adherence to His commands. This one comes to light when I sit down to spend time with God or read the Word and I find myself thinking 'What is the right way to do this so God is pleased to see me?' and 'What's the formula?'

Fear and guilt: Feeling fearful of God's judgment and guilty for not meeting His expectations, leading to a strained relationship. It's like a constant cloud of fearing you're just not good enough, and when things go wrong, it's a punishment from heaven.

I once had a pastor tell me I could experience a nasty fate if I didn't obey him – effectively telling me that God would take my life because of my perceived disobedience. Fear certainly grabbed my heart in that moment. I'm sure there are many more examples that you can think of.

Traits of a Father–child relationship with God

Unconditional love: Recognising that God's love for us is not based on our performance but on His nature as a loving Father. Sounds easy, but it's something I believe many of us, if not all, have struggled with at some point in our walks with Him. Knowing that you don't have to perform in any way for Him and that He is always pleased to see you will transform how you approach your times with Him.

Intimacy and trust: Building a relationship with God based on trust, where we can share our deepest fears, hopes and dreams with Him.

I have shared a little of one of my rawest moments with God, and I have to say, it was not pretty. I'm sure that the air turned blue at points, but I never once felt God was angry, quite the opposite. Once I had finished 'kicking off' in spectacular fashion and collapsed exhausted on the bed, I was clothed in an inexplicable peace from heaven, such is the love and grace of our Father.

Grace and mercy: Understanding that God's grace and mercy are always available to us, even when we fall short.

I don't know about you, but when I've messed up and have 'fallen short' I tend to have a need to feel guilty for a few days to prove how sorry I am. I 'hide in the garden'. Yet God wants nothing to separate us from Him. The blood of Jesus really is enough and we can keep very short accounts with God. He doesn't want us to hide. He wants to spend time with us and have nothing stand in the way; after all, that's why Jesus came.

The church that I am now part of have a lovely declaration that the children say in Sunday School. The first line is: 'I declare that God is always in a good mood.' How wonderful! God is always in a good mood. We don't have to test the water to second guess His reaction to us on any given day depending on what we've done. He is always in a good mood *and* He is always pleased to see us.

My heart's desire is that everyone reading this chapter would come into the glorious revelation of the true Father-heart of God and the freedom Jesus paid for us to walk in.

If you feel that you have struggled with a wrong perspective of our Father God, then don't be discouraged. The Holy Spirit is here and longing to reveal the truth to you. There are many resources available to help you on your journey of discovery, but a great place to start is quite simply: 'Daddy, help me', and He will be there.

15

Out of tragedy there is light

Carolyn's story

I always knew God was there… sometimes shown in the power of people around me… to do what they can, even when I say no because it's hard to say yes.

My wonderful son Tom took his life on the 29th of February 2024. I knew straight away that life for me would never be the same again. What I didn't know was what it would be like to grieve an adult child. But then who does? What I've learned is that there's no script, there's no right or wrong way, and that everyone's experience is different.

I want to put my experience on paper in the hope that it sheds light on my journey, that it acknowledges events that are both painful and joyful, and most importantly, it raises awareness of the impact of suicide, the impact of poor mental health and the challenges that young people face and their struggles to get to support.

I'm a fifty-something mum and granny, who I think has a good heart and a desire to help others. I have a strong sense of justice and an ambitious passion about people having a voice. I have a faith in God and I believe in God, even when He seems a long way away.

So who am I? I'm mum to a beautiful daughter, a wonderful son and a granddaughter. I sometimes talk too much, I'm slightly scatty, and I can be direct. I laugh at my own jokes, and I love being around family and friends. I enjoy the theatre, walking with my very naughty dachshund, and reading, singing, fine dining, good wine and stoolball. If you don't know what that is, look up Stoolball England!

I'm a social worker who qualified later in life. Yes, a social worker who advises parents and young people, yet couldn't 'social work' my own son – something I grapple with every single day.

Tom (Thomas) Guy Brockman was born on the 23rd of October

in the year 2000, younger brother to Jennifer who adored him from the moment he arrived. He was a small baby born at just 6 lbs and 1 oz and he was quite hairy. The midwife said he was like a little monkey! Tom was a quiet, calm and relatively contented baby who slept lots and continued to do so throughout his life. He was an amazing sleeper, sometimes too much in his later years. Tom had a keen love of all animals, especially monkeys and apes, and he loved Toy Story too. He was gentle, he was funny, kind and sensitive. He loved being around his friends, yet he didn't love school so much, but he carried on going despite this and despite it being hard.

At home he lacked confidence in himself, and post-2019 he became more anxious and somewhat depressed. He seemed to lack purpose. I felt he had no direction. He went to university at the start of lockdown and deferred because it wasn't what he had hoped it would be. He certainly found it difficult to motivate himself to study on his own and was a classroom learner.

Tom left and moved to London where he happily went to work in the fashion industry. However, he rapidly hit a low in December 2023, and he came back home to live with me. He picked himself up, or so it seemed, and found a job in Urban Outfitters where he'd worked previously in Tunbridge Wells. He seemed to be enjoying it and got back into the pattern of working and I believe was in a happier place for him.

On the 28th of February he called me at work at 10am when I was in a meeting. He wanted to tell me that had been paid but he hadn't been paid what he'd expected and he was very flat about it. I reassured him not to worry and that it was likely he was being emergency taxed, but I was quick on the phone because I had a meeting to go back to. That was the last time I spoke to Tom.

Later in the day, I received a call from his workplace to say he'd left a note on the desk saying he just had to leave and said he was sorry and he would explain later. I then received a call from my previous landlords to say the police have been there, asking about Tom. Tom had made a call. At that point, I started to panic. I tried to call Tom endless times, and he didn't pick up the phone. I messaged him and I went to Urban Outfitters and frantically ran around Tunbridge Wells with my colleagues looking for him.

I was then told by the police I needed to return home to meet them at our flat, which I did. I remember driving through the traffic....there was so much traffic, and I couldn't get home quickly enough. I received a further call from the police to ask if Tom had links to High Brooms, the very place I had been driving through. I told them that I didn't think so unless he was on the train. Tom still liked getting the train.

The police came to the house; they had had a call, but they wouldn't tell me what the call had said. They searched the flat, including Tom's room, took his toothbrush for DNA, and asked me to go and check the garage. I remember walking to the garage and getting to the door and thinking I couldn't open it. So, I had to ask the police officer to open it and look in the garage. The relief to see that he wasn't in there was enormous and it gave me hope.

However, as time moved forward, a post was put on the internet to say Tom was missing, which spread thanks to social media. It became very scary, as I became increasingly desperate. I was told by the police I needed to remain at home. Search parties were organised by Jennifer, my amazing daughter, his sister.

So many friends started to search. I remember my nephew came down from Leeds, my niece from London with her partner. Throughout the night, the police seemed absent. It was such a long night. We focused our search on the Powdermills area where we used to live, but it was so dark, so quiet and we couldn't find anything.

At three o'clock in the morning, Tom transferred money to my bank account. Jen and I called the police to tell them he was still alive and ask for someone to call me but I didn't receive a call. We rang again and again.

At seven in the morning, my daughter and I got in the car to drive to the police station because nobody had called us. On the way, we met our local PCSO on the road. Jennifer ran to her and she immediately rushed back to the police station with Jennifer because she didn't know about Tom. It was at that point Jennifer started to organise a search party while I went home and waited. Thanks to social media and local kindness, a huge number of people congregated to search for Tom.

I don't remember the next four hours, but *Ro sat with me, and this is her account:*

We sat waiting, just waiting....for any news, anything. Dread increased as time ticked by, and we just sat on the sofa, close yet rigid and frankly terrified at what might be... Two young police officers came to search the flat, support Carolyn, just to be there with her. So young yet so kind. Carolyn wanted to go out searching but they were firm she had to stay home.

Carolyn then had a call to ask what Tom's favourite place had been locally, and it was then that she knew where he was. She just wanted to go there, but they told us to stay put while they went to that place. We all knew that Jennifer and the search party were close to that location; they rushed off there.

The two police officers came back a short while later, to gently tell Carolyn what she had guessed, that Tom had indeed taken his life. How do you comfort a friend who is being told her life is being torn apart? That the worst you can imagine has just happened? Carolyn was inconsolable and I was scared for her; I didn't know what to do. I rang the GP to ask if someone could help, if a doctor could give her something to calm her down. I was told the doctors were too busy and to make an online application for support via 111; I was speechless.

Back to Carolyn:

How did we not work it out that night? I keep asking myself.

There was so much conflict around the funeral, the differences in what we all wanted. However, looking back, the people I met on my journey before and through and after the trauma, are the ones who have faithfully prayed for me and held me through it. For example, Sharon, whom I'd met 18 months before, who became the mediator, the organiser of Tom's thanksgiving service – she held it all together for us. God knew beforehand who I would need in my life to support me through this time.

I had a small group of friends I'd met after the trauma of divorce, and they held me. People from my old church rallied, in a way I hadn't expected. Faithful Christians who have prayed and helped me practically. Even my local Baptist Church – a church I didn't go to –stepped in.

For me, on reflection, I can now look back and see a ring of love and support surrounding me. I've realised people do love me and God loves me, as sometimes in my messy life, I have felt very unloved.

At Tom's funeral, I could see how much Tom was loved, but

people came to support me and Jen too. People sang, and it was so beautiful at the service, knowing there was a Christian community around it. I wanted that! Somehow, God enabled it. An old friend, Jon, who also loved Tom, came from Norfolk to do the talk. What I had thought wasn't going to be a Christian funeral became a Christian one, and it felt really safe.

Those people haven't gone away; they have stood with me, challenged me and I knew God was there. He is back; I'm now seeking out God more. I love the fact I've bought myself a large print Bible. I love to touch it, read it and enjoy it. It's been really fundamental. I don't put it away now, it lives out....there.

I see God in the mess now, I talk to him more. I'm a bit less angry with God. But I'm desperate to have one more chat with Tom.... Stop the clock. But I think this journey goes on...I have to do something positive with this journey even though there are dark days.

Does this shock you? What shocks me sometimes is, if I could be anywhere, where would I be? Heaven of course, as I want to be with Tom. It has been a challenge for me to believe he is in heaven. I do believe that. Tom asked to be baptised at the age of six, nearly seven. Before he died, he was reading his Bible and praying. He knew God.

I know I have to run the race, and I am so blessed to have Jennifer and the most wonderful joy-giving granddaughter. They keep me alive. Molly was a miracle baby, and she is an amazing gift. Tom loved Molly so much. God knew I needed her in my life.

I look at the blessings I have – my family, my friends, my new church – and none of this is possible without God. Every day is a sad day in some ways, but I am alive and I laugh and smile and I talk to God a lot. Every day it is getting better: from minus five out of ten a year-and-a-half ago, I'm now on six or seven.

The balance between space to be still and grappling with day-to-day life is a challenge. I'm trying to build more of God into life because it was God on pause for a while. Yet I saw God in the love of friends and unknown people, even the funeral organisers, and people who knew me by virtue of Tom who were so kind.

These verses are really important to me:

> The Spirit of the Sovereign LORD is on me,
> because the LORD has anointed me
> to proclaim good news to the poor.

He has sent me to bind up the broken hearted,
 to proclaim freedom for the captives
 and release from darkness for the prisoners,
to proclaim the year of the LORD's favour
 and the day of vengeance of our God,
to comfort all who mourn, and provide for those who grieve in Zion –
to bestow on them a crown of beauty
 instead of ashes,
the oil of joy
 instead of mourning,
and a garment of praise
 instead of a spirit of despair.
They will be called oaks of righteousness,
 a planting of the LORD
 for the display of his splendour.
Isaiah 61:1–3 (NIV)

The trauma for Tom was huge, and young people's mental health support was not enough, and it's needed. People are rightly advocating for this.

My energy is now focused on giving back something to support others in a way I have been supported. My vision is to develop supper for survivors. Perhaps to have a meal where people can eat and share and feel looked after and given a voice in an informal setting – mutual support.

16

Fruitfulness in brokenness

Kemi's story

I grew up in a large family in Lagos, Nigeria. My parents were both divorcees; dad had six children with his first wife and Mum had four children with her first husband. I came along as the first of three children following their remarriage.

My memory of growing up was one of living in a large house with a big compound and a constant stream of lots of different people of various ages coming and going. There was a cacophony of sound: loud music blaring from my siblings' rooms; music from the piano in the hallway; various conversations happening all at the same time, between us children, amongst my parents and their guests, housemaids and other helpers. Just so many people in the house, with the beautiful aroma emanating from the kitchen at all hours reminding me that our home was not just mine but belonged to many others who found it a welcoming place.

Amid all of these – people, order, chaos, noise, comfort – I found my escape in the world of dreaming with my toys. I was especially captivated by my dolls and kitchen appliances. Playing with my toys would take me to a future yet unknown. I would let my imagination run wild, pretending to be an adult in my own home cooking for my family, setting a table for my husband and children. This was a picture that was deeply rooted in my heart, a vision of the family I presumed I would have one day; three children running around the house laughing, playing and doing all the things children do in the midst of the chaos and the delight of being in a family.

Many years down the line, in my early thirties, I got married and my husband and I decided to travel the world as a couple before starting our family. Exploring the world together was a great adventure and it helped us immensely in getting to know each other better, adjusting to our diverse backgrounds, upbringing, personalities and cultures. Nearly three years after getting married and within a few months of trying for a baby, I became pregnant and I was ecstatic. The pregnancy was uneventful until the later stages where I got some negative news about the baby's growth but all was fine at delivery, thankfully. Although my heart and body had been anticipating the arrival of my son, coming face to face with him and holding him in my arms was such an amazing experience, as it evoked depths of love, joy and delight for him that I had not expected. I would whisper words of affection to my newborn son, sing to him, talk to him as I breast fed him during what became a special time of bonding between us.

As someone who was very much career-focused, I was surprised but incredibly happy when, within a few weeks, I had settled nicely into this new phase of life with all the learnings and routines that came with having a baby. I remember when my son was about six months old, my husband and I had a conversation about trying for another baby. We both laughed about the sleepless nights and concluded that, whilst we were really delighted about the joy of becoming first-time parents, it was best to wait before trying for another baby. Never did it cross my mind that my dream of having three children was not going to happen and that my son would be my only child. The story that I wrote for myself as a little girl has been rewritten; life has happened, with its interruptions, unexpected twists and detours.

I went back to work after eight months of maternity leave and found motherhood enjoyable and exhausting at the same time. I took my son with me to work, as my employer had a nursery that was available for employees and members of the public. The proximity of the nursery made life so much easier – seeing my son in the day and celebrating all the different milestones: rolling over, crawling, walking, smiling, cooing, babbling, saying words and waving 'bye was priceless.

When my son turned two, the journey of trying for another baby started. Days became weeks, weeks became months and months stretched into years. At the start of trying for another baby, during the doctor's appointment, I was told, 'Getting pregnant takes time, you need to give it time; relax or your body will not respond positively; eliminate stress', and all the other good advice given to aid fertility. When it became clear that I wasn't getting pregnant naturally, I was referred to a fertility clinic. I remember our visit to the clinic on Harley Street in London. The receptionist was nice enough, the waiting room was white and clean, full of couples with different leanings but united in their desire for a child, in a place that was sterile and cold.

Going through the process of finding out what was wrong and needed fixing was tough. We were ushered into a room and asked to do the needful so that samples could be collected and analysed. My heart ached but I was hopeful and longed for the day that I would be pregnant again. In the midst of it all I would have some challenging moments when I would be assailed by tormenting thoughts like, 'You are a woman and you can't even have a child. All normal women have children, there is something wrong with you!' I would cry to the Lord and ask 'Can you give us a child? What will it take for you to give us a child? Why is this not happening for us, what is wrong with us?' During the challenging times, I also found great comfort in pouring out my heart before the Lord and His peace and presence was always so tangible to me.

On one hand, whilst going through all of this, I was tight-lipped and kept a brave exterior, juggling all the demands on me as a female leader, mother, wife, minister and dealing with the pain of the brokenness from an unrealised desire. I had people say to me, 'We know you are all loved-up, don't you think it's time to have another child?' I would just smile and say, 'Pray for us.' But I never really spoke about it.

I found it hard to express my feelings of sadness, shame, failure and embarrassment about not been able to do what normal couples do – procreate. As I look back now, I realise that these were all lies of the enemy that I believed. On the other hand, I prayed for people and they got pregnant and I was also always so happy when friends announced the news of their pregnancies, because in my mind it was just a matter of time before I would get pregnant and there were more than enough babies in heaven to be released to the earth. So I made room in my heart for the children that I believed were coming.

We were eventually given a diagnosis of unexplained infertility which was difficult to get my head around as I had expected that once we knew what was wrong, we could seek treatment and deal with it. The realisation that my dream of having another child was unlikely to happen, was like a deafening silence – so many unanswered questions, shattered dreams. My desire and hope for my son to have siblings gone. It drove me to my knees. I ran to God, I had no back-up plan, there was no succour outside of Him.

I was completely helpless and felt so inadequate and this inadequacy drew me closer to God. I needed to have His validation as my notion of my identity had been wrapped up in ability or inability to have more children. Whilst I professed that my identity was in Him, I realised that there was a misalignment as I had allowed myself to be defined by my circumstances rather than by God. As I allowed Him to sing over me and draw me to a closer level of intimacy with Him as my Father, labels that I allowed to be put on me began to come off and I saw that I am complete in Him with or without more children. I was brought to a place of complete and total reliance on God.

Countless prayers continued and then one day I just knew that I needed to come to a place of rest where it did not matter whether I had another child or not. Prior to this time, I had gone to Florida for a three-day Christian event, 'Healed for Life', a ministry run by a lady called Jo Naughton. In the course of the event, I experienced deep inner healing as the love of God washed over me. Each session spoke to my heart powerfully and the Holy Spirit encountered me in such a profound way at ministry times that by the end of the event I knew that something in me had shifted and I experienced a new level of inner peace and joy.

It was during this new normal when my son was preparing for his GCSE exams that I felt a stirring in my heart to start a prayer group. In my local church, we had embarked on our annual 21-day prayer and fasting programme and, on one of the nights, a preacher had shared a message about turning your scars into stars. At the time, I wasn't overly taken by the title but as I listened I realised there was an opportunity here to turn something painful into something fruitful and 'The Seeds of Greatness' was sown into my heart. I heard the phrase dropped into my spirit and when I took my son to a meeting at his intended boarding school, whilst waiting for him during his interview, I walked into one of the school halls and inscribed on the wall was 'Seeds of Greatness'.

I kid you not, I was stunned and a little shaken but it became confirmation for me to start the prayer group. I said 'Lord, I am grateful to you for giving me my child, help me as I start the Seeds of Greatness prayer group, that as we pray every child will fulfil your plans for their life and I thank you for making me a mother of many.' My prayers completely changed from asking the Lord for a child, to asking the Lord for fruit to come out of my brokenness. I have found comfort and pleasure instead of the ache and pain that was in my heart.

We started in February 2017 after I shared my heart with some friends. I told them I was unsure how it would pan out, but I am going to take a step of faith to start the prayer group. Each time we gather virtually we read Scriptures and pray for all the children, (known and unknown) we carry in our hearts, our own children and their friends, children within our extended family, church, school, society at large and others that we would never meet on this side of eternity.

Our prayers were heartfelt, crying out to God to intervene in their lives. Word spread about our prayers, other mothers joining and bringing along their friends and we haven't looked back, each person with their own unique story of joy and pain from parenting. What was once a group of about ten mothers has now become a group of nearly one hundred parents (mothers and fathers) in different countries praying for their children, children within the body of Christ and the world at large.

I have become a mother of many as I have prayed for so many of 'my children'. We have cried and laughed together, carrying each other with our prayers, had testimonies of so many amazing things God has done and is doing in impossible situations ranging from relational, spiritual, professional, physical, mental, health issues and the list goes on. While not all our prayers over the children have been answered in the way that we wish, we can rest in the peace and truth of God's word that everything is working together for the good of those who love God and are called according to His purpose.

Looking back at the last eight years, I see how God has rewritten my story into something much more beautiful than I could have envisaged. I have discovered the joy of beauty in brokenness. Whilst I do not have another child, there is a level of joy that I am encountering that is allowing me to give life to others through my testimony, prayers and encouragement.

Although what I perceived to be and was intended to bring me shame and silence, my voice has led to freedom and so much joy and fulfilment in my life. Pain has been turned into purpose.

Yes, I still only have one child naturally but, through my situation, God opened a door that is touching many other lives and has made us as a family a part of many families. My son tells me he is so blessed to have mothers and fathers who pray over him and his generation. Infertility did not get the final word; God's redemption in the brokenness does. He is in the midst of my mess and making the mess better.

> So we are convinced that every detail of our lives is continually woven together for good, for we are his lovers who have been called to fulfil his designed purpose.
> Romans 8:28 (TPT)

17

Pride...and a drop in status

Grant's story

'Pride will cost you everything but leave you with nothing.'

A sobering thought, isn't it? One that has echoed in my heart many times. It came alive to me one cold February morning in 2017 as I walked through Finsbury Park. The air was damp and biting, the sort of London chill that seeps into your bones. Commuters hurried past with coffees in hand, coats buttoned tight, eyes fixed on the day ahead. I too was moving with purpose, heading towards Angel Tube station, when I noticed him.

He sat slumped against the wall, cross-legged, his frame thin and weary. A flimsy sleeping bag, little more than a sheet, was draped loosely across his shoulders. His lips were blue from the cold, his hands trembling as he gripped a piece of cardboard. On it, in faint, almost illegible writing, were the words: 'Hungry. Please help. Food or hot drink.' His eyes, hollow yet searching, met mine for the briefest of moments.

Earlier that morning I had been with a client who is also a good friend. We had spoken not only about business but about God. We had touched on His goodness, His love, His glory. Those thoughts lingered in my mind as I passed this man. I registered his condition. I felt the tug. But still, I kept walking.

And then came the conviction. With every step, it grew heavier. The Spirit whispering: 'Stop. Turn back. This is the "one".'

Tears sting my eyes even now as I recall it, because I too had once been in a place of deep brokenness. Not without a roof over my head, not without family or friends, but spiritually lost. Fallen. Empty. Searching. I had known what it was to tumble from the illusion of success into the reality of failure. I had known what it was to experience a 'drop in status', and I suspected that perhaps this man had too. Maybe he once had a career. Maybe he once had dreams. Maybe he'd fled his country in hope of a better life.

Whatever his past, whatever his story, he was still a child of God, my brother. Titles and positions may elevate us in the eyes of men, but they do not define us before God. Recognition cannot give peace. Success cannot give identity.

So I turned back. Retracing my steps, I approached the bus shelter where he sat, knees drawn to his chest. I crouched down beside him, lowering myself until I was at his level. His English was broken, but hunger speaks louder than words. I ducked into a nearby café, bought him a sandwich and a hot drink, and placed them into his hands. His eyes softened as he murmured thanks.

I don't share this to sound noble, to draw attention to myself, or to paint the picture of a modern-day good Samaritan. I share it because it reminded me of something vital: Jesus always stopped for the one. For the woman at the well. For the blind man on the roadside. For the bleeding woman who touched His cloak. For me. For you. And if I am to follow Him, then I too must learn to stop, to go low, to extend love where it is most needed. That morning was a small reminder. But my own story with pride, and the painful lessons I learned, runs much deeper.

It was September 2009. Some close friends were preparing to emigrate to Australia, and I joined them for a farewell gathering. We laughed, celebrated, toasted their new adventure. Yet just days earlier, I had stood in my office and with reckless arrogance declared myself 'untouchable'. A superhero. Invincible.

The words may have sounded like banter, but they revealed the truth of my heart. Pride had taken root. I had clawed my way into a senior position in that company not by integrity or steady diligence but by arrogance, self-promotion, greed, and a hunger for recognition. I wanted the title, the salary, the influence. And I got it, but without the character to sustain it. I lacked integrity. I lacked identity. I lacked foundation. And so, inevitably, came the fall.

That same week, I was struck with what felt like a kidney infection. The pain was relentless, like knives twisting in my side. For weeks I suffered, but test after test returned inconclusive. My doctor dismissed it as stress and suggested exercise, but I knew in my gut there was more. Anxiety began to coil around me like a snake. Fear gnawed at me day and night.

The months that followed were among the darkest of my life. I underwent tests for cancer – stomach, testicular, prostate – scans for kidney disease, endless bloodwork. Each time the waiting was torture. And each time the results came back clear. Nothing. No explanation for the pain. My body ached, but even more so my soul. I was unravelling.

By the winter of that year, I found myself in a clinic not meant for me at all, one that primarily treated sexually-transmitted diseases. Desperation had driven me there, chasing any possible thread of clarity. I was broken, hurting, stripped of dignity.

And then it happened. Sitting across from a Nigerian consultant, I blurted out words that surprised even me: 'I'm a Christian. I have a faith.' He laid down his pen, looked me in the eye, and asked: 'Well then… what are you doing here?'

His voice was calm but carried authority. What followed was not medical advice but a sermon – short, simple, piercing. His words cut through the fog of fear that had shrouded me for months. It was as though heavy clouds parted, and sunlight poured in.

Suddenly I saw it. For half a year I had tried to control every detail of my life. I had gripped tighter and tighter until my knuckles were white. And in the process, I had lost sight of the One who had never let go of me. In that sterile, fluorescent-lit room, I surrendered. I released my clenched fists and whispered, 'Father, I let go. Lead me. Take this. Do what You need to do in me.' It was the beginning of my healing.

That moment marked a turning point. Years earlier I had begged God to use me, but how could He when pride still consumed me? How could He when I was on a path of self-destruction? Stripped of status, I was finally ready to begin again. Not as a finished article, but as a disciple. An apprentice.

And that is what I remain to this day, an apprentice of Jesus. Still learning. Still stumbling. Still being shaped. God, in His mercy, has given me a teachable heart and a spirit that longs for His compassion. I still make mistakes. I still falter. But I know this: He is always there to pick me up, to dust me off, to set me walking again.

The greatest lesson I have learned? Pride will ruin everything. Pride whispers that we are enough on our own. That success, wealth and recognition will define us. That we can control our destiny. But it is a lie. Pride isolates, blinds and eventually destroys.

Humility, however, leads to life. Character and integrity are what truly matter. Not the trophies or promotions that line a CV. And character, as the saying goes, is who you are when no one is watching.

If we desire the right things, if we hunger for Jesus, for humility, for love, then our lives will overflow into our families, our communities, even our nations. A drop in status is not a loss; it is an opportunity. An opportunity to lift others up. To exalt the One who saved us. To find true joy and true purpose.

Looking back, I see how much I lost: status, confidence, control. Yet in losing those things, I gained what is infinitely more valuable. I discovered the joy of stopping for the 'one'. The freedom of surrender. The power of humility. There is no treasure, no wealth, no recognition greater than this: to be called a son of God.

> Humble yourselves before the Lord,
> and He will lift you up in honour.
> James 4:10 (NLT)

18

The uninvited guest

Bea's story

Depression is horrid. It's an unwelcome guest; it's an uninvited guest. No one who has suffered with it wants to entertain it. Comments like 'Pull yourself together', or 'You'll feel better after a good night's sleep', fall way short of even a hint of encouragement or support. But if you've never experienced it, it is hard to understand what it does to its host. If you are suffering with it, you are not alone. There are others who understand and still others who have successfully evicted the uninvited guest.

My story, exemplified in three separate insights, years apart, gives a taste of the unwelcome life I was living, until...

As a child I had a strange experience: sitting on the end of my bed with an inexplicable sensation of heaviness in my gut, or was it my heart? Maybe my mind? A deep sob rose up from this inner place and my body began to shudder as I cried for no apparent reason. I was barely a teenager, and I do not recall all the details, but these words from my mum I do remember: 'You've got the holiday blues.'

I didn't fully understand her explanation, yet it made sense to my young mind. The anticipation and excitement of a family holiday abroad was now over and the everyday routine of home life did not compare. But why was I crying, really crying? This wasn't some whimsical longing to return to a fun holiday environment. This was deeper. I could feel a cold vacuum in the pit of my stomach, which then clouded my mind and swept through my emotions, causing me to sit and sob.

Some years later: 'You're burnt out.' This was the summation of the doctor I had visited after my body had finally given up on me and I was incapable of working, or much else for that matter. She signed me off for two weeks with depression and prescribed antidepressants. 'Depression?' I'm not depressed; my body is just totally worn out, or so I thought.

I didn't want to be labelled as depressed and seemingly crazy. Rather, it was like a misfiring of various connections in my body, akin to putting my foot on the accelerator of a car and nothing happening; there was nothing left inside me. But depression? I don't think so! Yet as I began to speak to selected people about what had happened to get me to this point, they too concluded that it was depression. The idea of what I thought this condition was, was different to my reality. Like it or not, I was suffering with it.

And then: I stand and stare at myself in the mirror, my body devoid of energy and motivation. Knowing that it is going to take *all* the strength I have to get myself ready and into work is a desperate feeling that I do not want to have, at all, ever. Yet here I stand.

I get myself into work; on auto-pilot, driving on all-too-familiar roads. I get into the office and close the door. I stand by the window, my head in my hands, tears falling from my eyes as I wonder how on earth I will get through the day. In reality I know I can't, but somehow, I do. I got through the day. I came home as early as I could, then just lay on my bed, looking at Twitter, watching the world do its thing – more like staring at something alien, something I'm not really part of. I'm an alien on my own planet!

Four-thirty pm and I'm in bed. Far too early to go to sleep but I am *so* tired. I could fall asleep but then I'd wake up stupidly early. So, I force myself to stay awake. My body clock is out of sync; physically I'm creaking due to lack of rest and sleep. A helpful and kind colleague who supported me today sent a message which ended with, 'Do not think about tomorrow until tomorrow.' Yeah, tomorrow. Each day is different. Hopefully it will be easier to get up tomorrow.

Depression can often leave us with more questions than answers: Why me? What's wrong with me? Why can't I cope? Why don't others struggle? I questioned myself incessantly. I've been furious, aghast, incandescent, incredulous, bemused, flummoxed, disappointed and totally at a loss as to 'Why me?'

Regardless of whether depression is rooted in emotions, trauma, a chemical imbalance or something else, one thing never changes: the truth that Jesus Christ is our healer. He is the One who can redeem all things. Nothing is bigger than or superior to Almighty

God, therefore our feelings, past, trauma, circumstances and anything we think the devil or someone else has done to us, bows its knee to Jesus. Herein lies the key to gaining healing and freedom from the uninvited guest.

I encountered God and became a Christian in my late teens and steadily grew in my love and understanding of Him and the Bible. Yet the thread of depression ran continuously through my life. When unfathomable lows hit, God seemed distant and my faith was like a fog that acted as a heavy blanket over my thoughts and feelings.

During adulthood, I had reached crucial junctures when depression obscured reality. This included a physical, emotional and mental burnout that left me incapable of functioning 'normally'. The simple reality was that I could not cope. Work, relationships, eating and sleeping were all fractured. This had led me to seek counselling and then a Christian retreat where I was graced with the time, space and prayer to allow God to pick out the debris of depression and begin to piece me back together.

Yet, what I did after recovering was to think, wrongly, 'I've been healed of depression. I don't need to do anything. It's gone; I can get on with my life.' But then, when a difficult situation arose, instead of standing on the truth of Scripture and applying it, I reverted back to dealing with it and processing it through my emotions and limited understanding. In other words, I still relied on me. But by relying on myself instead of the word of God, depression was able to latch onto a part of me once again and take up residence.

Even with a strong faith, I was weak. When life was going well, this lack was not so noticeable, but when challenges came, the cracks were evident. During times of being over-busy, my prayer, worship and Bible-reading times diminished. I wasn't filling myself with the spiritual nourishment that was necessary to stay healthy and as a result, how I felt would effectually take over. I wasn't using the weapons at my disposal, such as verses of Scripture, to face up to the attacks.

Being a Christian is an ongoing process, every day, and I needed to feed myself responsibly with God's word. Yet, because my default in difficult times would be to rely too much on myself and how I felt, I wasn't adequately applying biblical truths. Reading them, yes, but not applying them.

One of the biggest battles I experienced was after a long-term relationship finished. It wasn't a mutual split and it hit me hard. This caused a massive downturn in my life. Depression was at its ugliest and I could not see a way through it. Yet, when I look back on this season (thanks to the journals I kept) there was time upon time when a Scripture, a song, or a word of encouragement would pop up out of the blue, like breadcrumbs leading me on the path back home, to Father God.

In Romans 8:28 it says: 'In all things, God works for the good of those who love him.' (NIV) Throughout it all, He was (and is) there.

Ultimately, I was able to attend an inner healing course, and it proved to be the fatal blow to the uninvited guest. Daily times of teaching, confession and prayer, identified and exposed the root of the depression. With one final time of prayer and deliverance, it was eliminated. It was tough to do but the determination to be free was overriding and so worthwhile. Years of questioning, of damning myself, were finally gone. Depression had left the building!

If we focus on the depression it wins. The real and deep struggle is having the energy to stand and remain standing; to fight for the truth to reign supreme in our hearts and minds. I know first-hand that it is not easy. I know how difficult and isolating it is. I know how pathetic and embarrassing it feels having to admit to yourself and to others that we are 'less than' them, 'less than' the norm. It is incredibly demeaning. But continually aligning ourselves to depression weakens our resolve and trust in who God is and who we are in Him. Therefore, stand we must.

Ask at least one person to stand with you. Have a word or key phrase that you can text them when the going gets tough, so that they know to pray for you. Keep declaring God's word; keep confessing who He is and not what you are not. Depression is beatable because Jesus has already defeated it! The battle is in the mind, but we have the mind of Christ and we have the ability to take thoughts captive. The key thing is to believe these words are true and live them out on a daily basis.

> We demolish arguments and every pretension that sets itself up against the knowledge of God, and we take captive every thought to make it obedient to Christ.
> 2 Corinthians 10:5 (NIV)

19

Who likes to be broken? Nobody!

Ania's story

Growing up in a society where life's difficulties were one of those accepted parts of everyday situations and routines in Poland, I used not to think much about joy. Yes, I had many joyful moments, but the seriousness of the situations of those I helped and in my own family, made me aware that problems and their complexities are what we need to concentrate on.

God did not give up on me with the subject of joy. One day as I was taking communion He whispered in my heart: 'I suffered so you would have *joy!*' Obvious, but this time it just jumped out to such a new and a strong level that I knew this 'exchange' was from Him. Even more, that joy was for me. I started to wonder 'What did this mean in my present reality?'

My life still seemed to be in pieces after my divorce, the first one in our family, and I also lost the possibility of a great business, leading to financial ruin, yet amazingly, a charity was formed from this time of pain. In the midst of it came joy. As I fasted one day, God urged me to read some articles about running a humanitarian charity to help children and families going back to their home country. It was great to see help given where it was needed but still this was not the centre of what brought joy to my life.

Did something else happen and change around me? No. One day I was trying to finish up the translation of a book for our conference, and I was just simply not able to do it. My computer kept giving up, and finally I said to God, 'I am trying to be faithful to you and finish it on time. So, help me, please!' Nothing changed with the computer; instead I heard, 'Go to the bookshelf and pull out the book which you brought from your time abroad.' The voice was clear and strong.

So that is what I did. I thought that this book would help me with the work I was doing with Holocaust Survivors. I really did not remember the title or know its content.

As I opened the first chapter, I realised that I wouldn't be getting back to work for some time, as I sat and allowed God to touch my heart, the past and the dreams I had had, my identity, and my current reality. I was in total shock and surprise! Shock that I was not able to stop what was happening with me, and surprise at how He came and knew what was in the deepest parts of my heart. We confronted my greatest fears together: my lack of finances, my loneliness. Every day I was able to read only one chapter. No work, just allowing Him to come behind the veil with me.

As I sat and read and prayed in the stillness with Him, a new me emerged, more beautiful and stronger than ever before. My broken heart was starting to heal as I realised the extent of His love. He is my beloved. I hid nothing from Him. People who seemed to have such normal lives, families and jobs started to want to be with me because of the joy and peace I had – simply because of Him. I stopped running around to help save everybody's lives, and instead I enjoyed being a daughter of a King. It was not just what was written in the Bible, but He wrote it on my heart and life.

God relates to each of His children in a way we can each relate to or understand. I read about ancient Jewish weddings. The knock at the door, like Jesus at the door, coming like the father of the bride comes to ask for the hand of the woman for his son. We have a decision to make – do we let Him in or not? I couldn't stop talking about God, but in a new way. It was about intimacy rather than me doing things.

I met Him in a way which changed my whole life, although I thought that I had known Him before. After one Shabbat, being with my Lord alone, looking at the day dawning, and the need to start the new week, one sentence came to my mind that summarised how I felt then and until now: 'Shabbat time is not enough, I need eternity to get to know my Beloved God. He is like a huge ocean, and I can swim little parts of it every day.'

For more than fourteen years I did not remarry. I had so much to do in life, and my family was growing. My daughter said to me one day, 'You must be happy, mum; are you? You laugh a lot, you have many friends, and so on.' This was the truth. Many of the difficulties continued but I was *just happy* with who I was, with my children and grandchildren, new challenges at the charity, meeting interesting people. Several times I replied 'No' to the opportunity of getting married. God, seeing me, and how much I love having deep relationships, did not give up on me. I was not looking for a relationship, but there came a time when I decided that I needed to pause. I wanted to be quiet with other people just listening to Him. So, I went to the Torah study at my friend's house. I was looking for God, but met not only Him, but also my present husband – a widower, as he shares in his own chapter of this book.

What is strange is that during the time when the war beyond our eastern border started, I had so much to do with those passing through our country to Israel, that normally I would not have time to get to know somebody. Life surprised me, and as I say now with Krzysztof, 'The war, love and the wedding come together'. He came along supporting me when I was tired. He prayed, brought food and talked with me. We talked and shared and shared, and in the end we fell in love with each other. You can probably gather from this story that I was not the youngest by this time. By a miracle I purchased a white dress, and after the ceremony we went to Kotel to pray. Suddenly, I looked at Krzysztof and said to him: 'Let's skip the taxi and walk through the town to our destination.' He agreed.

For the first time in my life, I understood much more why in the Bible joy is very often connected to 'The Bride and Groom'. We were so wonderfully surprised how many people in buses and cars stopped to say *'Mazal tov'* ('All the best' in Hebrew). Even those who walked with faces looking down to the ground, looked up and blessed us. And what was even greater for us: their faces lit up, like ours. What does it remind you of? Waiting for another great wedding!

> Hallelujah! For our Lord God Almighty reigns.
> Let us rejoice and be glad and give him glory!
> For the wedding of the Lamb has come,
> and his bride has made herself ready.
> Fine linen, bright and clean, was given her to wear. ...
> Then the angel said to me, 'Write this: Blessed are those who are invited to the wedding supper of the Lamb!' And he added, 'These are the true words of God.'
> Revelation 19:6–9 (NIV)

20

Not ready

Krzystzof's story

I should have been ready for the 'passing' from this earth of my wife Bogusia, due to her prolonged heart failure over many years and the very serious damage to her heart. But it seems I was not.

The doctors suggested that one more operation could help Bogusia and that a new part could be placed in her heart. As it happened, the pandemic struck, and they were not able to perform it. COVID made my wife even more sick and we had to put aside this option.

Suddenly, out of blue, a relative came from the south of Poland, a few hours from Warsaw where we were living, with the information that there was a clinic in the south of the country, where there was a famous professor who specialised in this type of operation, and it might be available on National Insurance. Our spirits rose, then abruptly dropped as my wife's sister announced that all the surgery slots had been taken. I don't know why I did what I did, but I got up, took the phone in my hand, and dialled the clinic asking for a place for my wife on the surgeon's list.

Bogusia was becoming much weaker, and I knew that help was necessary. The lady at the reception confirmed that there was a very long waiting list for the operation, and no possibility to help my very sick wife at the moment. To the surprise of all of us, the conversation didn't finish there. Instead, I was unexpectedly asked to wait. There was a silence on the phone and a long time of waiting. It seemed interminable. Then the voice on the other end, seemingly as surprised as me, said that my wife could come in tomorrow – I hadn't expected that response!

Another difficulty, or perhaps complexity to this, was that there were two types of the part which needed to be placed in my wife's heart. By a miracle, they very quickly found they were able to get the one which my wife preferred: the one that didn't need replacing every few years. We were amazed!

So, that evening, my wife went with her sister to the hospital in the south of the country and was taken initially for a thorough check-up of her general health. By this time, we were so used to procedures, it seemed like just one more along our journey. If something goes on for a long time, you get used to it. I'd been with her for so many hospital appointments and she'd always come home. We'd been together thirty-four years, and for half of this time we'd been told she wouldn't survive for long, yet she had. She had such trust and we kept praying.

We knew that her lungs were in bad condition after COVID, but still hoped for help. Again, to our total surprise, after the check-up, the doctors announced that her lungs were in perfect condition. Again, we praised God.

In addition to all those good results, we heard from this Polish-American clinic where the operation was going to take place, that nearby there was a convalescent home available for my wife to be able to get medical care for a while afterwards. What else could we desire? We trusted that this would be the way in which God would give Bogusia a few more years.

The operation went well. My wife woke up and was given some more medication to help her rest. She slept during the night, but in the morning her heart just 'broke'... this was the message. It couldn't cope with the new part.

This was so sudden. I was in such terrible shock. I felt as though I was completely going out of my mind. Before the operation I was asking God to perform a miracle in my wife's life, like He did in the life of Hezekiah: prolonging it for another fifteen years:

> Then the word of the LORD came to Isaiah: 'Go and tell Hezekiah, This is what the LORD, the God of your father David, says: 'I have heard your prayer and seen your tears; I will add fifteen years to your life.'
> Isaiah 38:4 (NIV)

What I did not understand at that time, but my wife's family doctor pointed out to me later on, was that God had performed what I had asked Him for already. After the death of my wife, the doctor concluded: 'For more than the last fifteen years, every day of Bogusia's life was a real miracle from God! With the condition of her heart and health in general, she shouldn't have lived for so many years.'

On top of the grieving that year, I was in three life-threatening situations. It seemed God wanted to keep me alive despite the circumstances. Firstly, as I drove through a green light, a large car went straight into my car. My car was a wreck but I was unscathed. Secondly, while out riding my bike, I crashed into a lorry. I was thrown off my bike onto the lorry, with a bang to my head and a shock to my spine, but again, no long-term consequences. Thirdly, when driving on the highway in the fast lane, I started to fall asleep and lost control of the car. To this day, I don't know how I survived!

I never thought that my life could be broken into pieces this way. That my life would just collapse in a moment: physically, emotionally, spiritually. I know I should probably have been ready for it, but I was totally *not!*

Adonai decided differently – He left me and took Bogusia to Himself instead. Every day, in my numbness, I would try to say two sentences as my prayer to Him. I wasn't able to do anything more. I trusted unconsciously that He heard them, and He would make them true in my life.

Those sentences are: 'God is good' and 'we know that in all things God works for the good of those who love him.' Romans 8:28 (NIV)

I believe that because of that, God healed my heart and gave me a 'new life'. Really new! What was incredible was that after several months, I stopped dwelling on the past and stopped wanting to complain to God. I felt I'd lost everything, even my beautiful home as we had given it in a will to our daughters. *But He gave me a new life!*

He lifted me out of wallowing in old memories. My daughter, who had her own grief over the loss of her mother, and my close friends helped me understand how to move forward. They encouraged me to stop looking in the direction of *death* and look towards the *life* which lies ahead. At some point, I'm not sure how it happened, I discovered that 'the old' just wasn't there anymore. This was unbelievable… even for me. Only God could have done it.

I am very thankful for, and respectful of, all my past life, even with my mistakes, but in carrying the pain and the 'old' I would not have been able to step out into God's 'new'.

I knew myself and recognised that life as a single man was not for me. I wanted to share it with someone close to my heart. As my heart got healed bit by bit, I started to slowly look around me. Shortly afterwards, God decided differently. He came to me and said: 'Leave it to me.' So I did, and allowed Him to continue healing my broken and still painful heart.

God gave me a wife of His heart – Ania, and a new life with her. My wounds were still in the process of healing. I noticed, for example, the entangling fear when my new wife was going to work or out to see her friends without me. I was scared that I would lose her too. She is a very busy, active person and has many friends, so at first it wasn't easy. Yet now we're at the point when we share more time together as well as doing things separately. The fear is gone. Praise to Him.

This was, I believe, due to the fact that when I met Ania, my hearing and talking with God 'came back'. For the first two or three months after my wife's death, I couldn't put two sentences together to say to God. I was in such shock, everything stopped. I didn't even ask 'Why, God?' I was numb.

However, with the help of friends, my life rebooted. It was a slow process. As I used to do before, I now pray constantly. Maybe in a different way, and not simply interceding. I enjoy walking with the Almighty every day, and not alone, but with Ania, my dear wife.

When the terrible death of Bogusia happened, I suddenly noticed that the builders had built a new road just next to our house. Instead of a small, narrow, road, among the houses and the forest, there was suddenly a very wide and paved road. I knew that through this picture, God was showing me to step out of the old into something different which He had placed in front of me; a new life after meeting Ania – a new life for us both.

21

How much cancer?

Nathan's story

I was in Canada. My uncle, my dad's brother-in-law, had just passed away on the 1st April 2024 and we gathered for his funeral. It was sad, but was also full of love, joy and support. My uncle and aunt had been well-known members of their local church, and so had developed a very strong relationship with the Pastor, who often referred to them as Mum and Dad. So it was just like a large family get-together.

It was on this trip that my phone rang with a call I didn't want to take. Being in another country I knew there would be a cost because the bill would run high, but I didn't realise just how much of a cost it would be. I didn't answer.

It was quickly followed up by a text. It was my Doctor's surgery. The message went something like 'Mr Curtis, we would like you to come in for a meeting with the consultant on such and such a date to discuss your biopsy.'

'Hmm,' I thought, It sounded a bit ominous. Anyway, I continued my trip to the US and back to Toronto, Canada and then finally back to the UK.

It was a Thursday morning, sometime in late April. I got to the surgery early as I normally do, and waited, also normal. There was a bit of a backlog. Finally, it was my turn. I sat in front of the consultant, and he asked if I knew why I was here. My mouth said nothing, but my brain was speaking loud and clear. 'You are asking me if I know why I'm here? How should I know? You called me!'

'Well,' he continued, 'it's regarding your biopsy; you've got cancer.'

Now, once again, my face didn't show it, and my mouth didn't say anything, but my brain started to go off again. Cancer? So, you're going to sit there and calmly, stoically, matter-of-factly tell me I have cancer? Where's the compassion? Where's the, 'Sorry mate, I don't know how to tell you this, or is there someone I can call?' Hmm, maybe that's too much of a stretch. But is it? Where's the empathy? It's not every day one sits in a surgery and hears the words no one ever wants to hear.

My doctor went on to say that this prostate cancer was extremely aggressive and action needed to be taken as soon as possible. It was actually stage 4. This indicates the cancer has spread to distant parts of the body, such as lymph nodes, bones or other organs.

He gave me two options: radiation therapy or surgery. He said that if they did radiation therapy and the cancer came back, then they would not be able to use that type of treatment again. But if I had surgery, and the cancer came back, they'd be able to use radiotherapy to treat it.

They gave me some literature to browse, although they could have easily pointed me to the internet because that's where I'd be getting most of my information from anyway. They also told me that I'd have to have a PET scan just to make sure that the cancer hadn't spread into the lymph nodes or to any other part of the body.

I then had to go home to let my wife, Sharon, in on this interesting turn of events. I would like to say here for the record, because I know people will be wondering: How did I feel when he told me about the cancer?

Good question. I was pretty calm, actually. I know some people are thinking, he must have been hysterical, dying on the inside. What traumatic news. Am I gonna die?

No, I was quite calm. This, I believe, was the first intervention of God's grace. That peace that passes all understanding, keeping my heart and mind and reminding me of who I am and whose I am. That peace settled on my heart; my mind began to think of eternity and the what-ifs. Was it my time? Had I done all that I was created to do?

So, interestingly enough, I was quite settled. As a believer, you've made your peace with God. Every day is a day to keep on walking in the peace of God as we are drawn into His presence. So, I was thinking on one hand, 'I can't wait to see Jesus,' and on the other hand, 'I've still got things to do. I've still got books to write, songs to write, people to speak to about Jesus.'

And then I had a family, a lovely wife and two daughters. What about them? So yes, I contemplated death, but by the grace of God, I was not fearful. I believe that God had prepared me in advance for that very time. About a year before, I would often wake up in the morning and hear the words 'You are healed'. I would respond to the Lord and say 'Yes, I know I'm healed'. Because at that time, as far as I was concerned, there was nothing wrong. I was fine, or so I thought.

Anyway, let me jump forward to going home to see my wife. She asked me how the appointment with the doctor went. I broke down the conversation as best I could. She sat there, shocked. It seemed to affect her more than it did me. 'I can't go into work tomorrow, there's no way,' she said. We sat there looking at each other, contemplating what this meant for the future. She told me to start again and go over every detail of the conversation – the good, the bad and the ugly.

To be honest, I think we were both in a state of shock, but we were coherent enough to agree on this one point. We would not broadcast this to everyone; however, we would speak to people whom we knew would pray. So that is what we did. We spoke to our house group leaders, my cousin and her husband, and one or two people in the prayer team at my local church.

It was absolutely amazing to have that prayer support. It felt like a warm blanket of God's love was surrounding me. I literally felt the power of prayer supporting me, holding me, energising me. So many people suffer in silence, maybe because they want to show the world how strong their faith is, or maybe because they have no one to talk to. At this point, I would like to really encourage you to surround yourself with believing believers. People who, when you say pray, will pray. Don't suffer in silence. That's one of the reasons God encourages us to fellowship with one another. I really saw the beauty of it in that season.

Coming from a pastoral background, where I'd been used to praying for everyone, I now saw and experienced first-hand the power of corporate prayer directed at my family and I.

Now, I had mentioned that the consultant at the hospital had said that he had wanted me to have a PET scan just to make sure that the cancer hadn't spread anywhere else in my body. This was organised for about a week later. This time, my wife went with me. The scan went as per usual, and they said that the surgery will be in touch with me in a few days.

They called me in and said, 'Mr Curtis, we have good news for you. The cancer has not spread to any other part of the body.' Good news indeed. There was one thing, though, he remarked, they found a shadow on your lung. Perhaps it's nothing. We certainly don't think it's related to the prostate cancer. Anyway, we'll refer you to the lung department, and they can look at it after we have dealt with the pressing issue, the prostate cancer.

Now I had to decide on which procedure I was going to have. To be honest, I had already made up my mind, but I needed to discuss it with my wife, who I knew would be in full agreement.

I decided on the surgery because I felt that the cancer was an intruder in my system and had to be dealt with radically. So that's what we went with.

The 11th June 2024, was the day. From the time I was diagnosed with cancer to the time of the surgery was approximately two months. I was in a good place, surrounded by prayer and the love of my family. I battled mentally about speaking to my dad, as he was my mother's carer and had a lot on his plate. But I thought if he ever found out from someone else, he would not be happy, so I informed him. My mother wouldn't have understood.

So, I had surgery to remove the prostate, which went well. No problems. They just put me to sleep, and that was that. I awoke, my prostate removed and I was looking forward to leaving. But I had to stay a while longer due to excessive bleeding and I saw it as an opportunity to talk with the other patients.

Three days later, I was released. Hallelujah! My wife and daughter came to pick me up as I wasn't allowed to drive or lift anything heavy for the next six weeks. But I was in very good hands, my family's and the Lord's.

The recovery went well, healing was fast, but there were side-effects of the surgery, some of which I'm still dealing with today. I won't go into that here, but I still believe that I am healed and that the manifestation of that healing will become evident shortly. Nothing is impossible for God.

Now, remember I said that I had to have a PET scan? Well, I was referred to the lung clinic and they told me that it didn't look like much, but they needed to check it out some more just to be safe.

They asked me, or rather booked me in, for another PET scan. This one was supposed to be more detailed than the one I had previously. 'Mr Curtis,' my consultant said, 'I have spoken to the consultants at Guy's hospital up in London, and they believe you have lung cancer. They are not 100 per cent sure, but it's serious enough for us to get you into surgery right away.'

What? Again? Gosh, what is going on here? My wife was with me this time, so she could ask all the questions that I couldn't. Once again, we were both stunned.

So, just barely recovering from a long four-hour surgery, I was to be going back, this time to a different hospital for another serious surgery. I know you are wondering how long after the first surgery was the second one. Well, it was approximately three-and-a-half months.

So I had to do more checks at the hospital. More prodding and the like. All through this, though, people were praying. I knew it, I felt it. I felt the peace of God that passes all understanding. I knew *He* was with me. Even though He wasn't speaking a lot, He was there and not just with me, but my whole family.

On the day of the surgery, my wife and I headed out in the early hours of the day. My sister-in-law booked a luxurious taxi for us. We felt like royalty. God was saying, 'I've got you, my son.'

We spoke to the anaesthetist, who explained to us all the ramifications of the surgery. There was something that he said that concerned me. 'We are going to have to collapse your lung, Mr Curtis.' Collapse my lung? Why didn't you tell me that before? Collapse my lung? Gosh. A fine time to be telling me that. 'Don't worry, Mr Curtis, we'll look after you.' Trust me, I thought, you have no idea who's looking after me!

Once again, the surgery went well, no hiccups at all. They found that it was cancer and had to take out a few sections of my left lung. But glory be to God, a few weeks later we discovered that they had got everything and no cancer remained.

Recovery from this surgery was a lot more painful, though. They told me afterwards that chest surgeries can be the most painful in recovery. They gave me all kinds of medications: paracetamol, oxycodone and morphine. After a while, nothing seemed to work, but then the Lord stepped in and gave me a seemingly irrelevant Scripture: ' LORD, by Your favour You have made my mountain to stand strong'. Psalm 30:7a (NASB)

I felt the power of God surge up my body, and the pain stopped. Thank God for our mighty God. He is my healer.

In November 2024, I was declared cancer-free. Hallelujah, thank you, Jesus! I still go for checks every three months, but I'm not expecting the cancer to return. When we trust in the Lord, He will not fail.

I hope you were encouraged by my story and that you would know that there is nothing impossible for our God. Sometimes he takes us out of the fire, and sometimes he walks with us through the fire. Either way, He is a God of miracles.

22

Anxiety replaced with certainty

Aparajita's story

> Do not be anxious about anything, but in every situation, by prayer and petition, with thanksgiving, present your requests to God.'
> Philippians 4:6 (NIV)

Paul isn't denying that life brings trouble, but he's urging believers not to be controlled by anxiety. This verse has encouraged me during the most trying times of my life. I am comforted knowing that God is there, and that I don't have to worry but instead, pray with a thankful heart and trust God with my needs.

This verse has spoken to me powerfully in times of deep personal pain. Sometimes, when our world is unravelling, it can be difficult not to be anxious and to surrender ourselves fully to God. The future feels uncertain, and the heart is raw. But God has always come through in times when I felt overwhelmed, with miracles happening every second of my life to keep me afloat in some of my most difficult moments.

A few years ago, my marriage went through a rough patch where I faced betrayal and heart-wrenching pain. I felt alone. A series of events happened which ultimately led to my divorce, and that broke me. Sometimes in life, one feels unsettled and questions everything. Despite going through that, I am able to look back and marvel at God's plan and how He carried me through troubled times as my guide and my Abba Father.

God does not ask us to pretend that everything is okay. Instead, He asks us to bring it all to Him. He invites us to shift where we place our focus, not on the worries and people around us but on Him. Even in the most unsettling times, He has not abandoned me. Circumstances don't change overnight, but gratitude shifts the atmosphere in our soul, enabling us to better deal with hardships.

I remember a time when I felt absolutely alone, in a new city and a new workplace, with not many people I knew. All my friends and family were far away, most of them thousands of miles away. Tonbridge was new to me, and I had recently relocated there from Manchester for job-related purposes. I have always felt God's blessings, mercy and grace upon my life since I can remember, even as a child. He has been there every step of the way, encouraging me, supporting me, and listening to my heart's desires even before I knew what was best for me.

He has blessed me immensely. I have been successful in my job and personal endeavours, and I have had a beautiful family and friends growing up, to share my joys and heartaches with. He has given me everything. Sometimes, when a storm hits us, we feel our foundation shaken and it becomes difficult to keep faith and surrender to God. But that's what true faith is; it demands this in the toughest of situations and seasons. Faith is like walking on water without fear, knowing God will not let us drown.

God came through at a time when I thought I was all alone, far from family and familiar faces. I remember waking up in the middle of the night with a racing heart, wondering how I would get through the next day. How would I be strong for others when I felt completely undone inside? I used to have panic attacks and would try to pace myself. It was in that place, not when I was strong, but when I was at my weakest, that Philippians 4:6 became more than just words to me. These words were breathing the living God.

Divorce leaves scars, yes, but it also became a space where God met me deeply. I never expected to write this chapter because divorce wasn't in the script I had hoped for in my life. I didn't suddenly become brave. I didn't suddenly 'let go and let God.' What I did was start small. I whispered prayers through tears. I wrote down the things I was scared to say out loud. I brought petitions to God – sometimes desperate, sometimes angry, always honest. He nursed me back. There were uncertain times when I wasn't sure about my job, whether I would be able to keep my home, or whether I could pay solicitor's bills. I saw in real time how God took care of me when I was in need. Things came through without asking; funds became available before I even knew I needed them.

God also gave me a wonderful and supportive church community where I could make friends and confide in others. He gave me much more than I desired and is continually bestowing His choicest blessings upon me every single day of my life. God's love has shone through the power of a loving and God-fearing community.

If one were to ask me what I am learning in my relationship with God, it would be to surrender my worries to Him and let Him take control of my life. He gives me motivation every day, protects me under His wings and showers me with His grace and mercy.

Also, I am learning the power of forgiveness and that how it helps one's healing can be profound. Another verse comes to mind:

> Bear with each other and forgive one another if any of you has a grievance against someone. Forgive as the Lord forgave you. Colossians 3:13 (NIV)

We forgive not from our own strength, but because we have been forgiven ourselves. This kind of forgiveness isn't a feeling; it is a decision we make every day and at every moment to walk in grace, even when we're hurt.

Growing up, I have memories of how essential prayer was in my life. I did have seasons when I became lax in my relationship with God; we all struggle with it to some extent. But I managed to find my way back to faith and trust in God's will for my life. I was blessed with a beautiful childhood, loving parents and grandparents. I fondly remember my grandpa. He was a devout Christian man with immense love for Christ, our Lord. A big part of my younger life was shaped by him. I remember the sermons he used to give at their local church. My mother is a prayer warrior whose powerful words and prophetic insights I have witnessed becoming true in real life.

I now reflect back and realise the impact my family had on my Christian life. I also realise how immensely blessed I have been to have a loving and supportive family and good Christian influence in my early days. This environment at home instilled qualities in me like gratitude, humility, empathy, and love for our brothers and sisters. I realised pretty early on the importance of living my life with God on my side.

There was another trying time in my life a few years ago when I underwent surgery and doubted whether I would be completely okay.

But I did get better, and I've almost forgotten that chapter of my life. Every time I was faced with a hurdle, I crossed it together with God.

I feel there have been so many blessings in our lives that if we truly start counting them, they would be uncountable. The thing is, in happier times, we fail to remember that God has been with us every step of the way. Sometimes, a period of suffering brings us closer to God. It's the soil where deep faith is grown:

> The LORD is close to the broken-hearted and saves those who are crushed in spirit. Psalm 34:18 (NIV)

Our pain never goes to waste. We sometimes pray out of routine, not out of pure dependence. The realisation that we need God to guide us in every aspect of our lives comes through hardship and suffering. God never said there would be no trials in our lives. But He does promise His *agape* love, sending His Son to atone for our sins. We are already forgiven in His mercy and grace.

I've found that praying like a small child has helped strengthen my relationship with God. I need no filter, just like how a child tells its parents things without thinking. God yearns for us to be His children and share with Him all the little things in our lives. He's there for all the nitty-gritty details: our fears, desires, let-downs, worries, interests, motivations, all of it! God's word is important. His is the only word that is constant and the rock in turbulent times. I'm learning to depend fully and wholly on that rock every single day.

There are so many miracles in my daily life that it's difficult to fully put them into words. I've found myself discovering I had been facing a problem only after it had already been resolved! Deep trust and dependence on the Lord are needed to live a truly fulfilling life. It might seem daunting and near impossible, but as one starts walking the path with full submission, it becomes more and more possible.

And while I may not have all the answers, far from it, I now walk with a heart full of gratitude, not because life is perfect, but because I know I'm never walking alone.

> Even though I walk through the darkest valley, I will fear no evil, for you are with me; your rod and your staff, they comfort me. Psalm 23:4 (NIV)

Every moment, every breakthrough, every tear and every triumph has reminded me that God's grace truly is sufficient. For that, I am forever thankful.

23

The reformation firehouse

Rebecca's story

I pulled into the driveway of my home in the middle of an afternoon after running errands. It was like any other day, but I will never forget this particular moment. Suddenly, I heard the voice of God. He said, 'Rebecca, do you feel that?' A little startled at breaking silence with the sound of His voice, I paused. 'Feel what, Lord?' I replied, while still thinking, pondering, and discerning the atmosphere.

I then responded with a questioning voice, wondering if I had the right answer, 'I feel peace?' 'Exactly, my daughter,' He replied. 'I had to strip the chaos out of you to show you what my true peace feels like.' I was in awe! Quite stunned, actually. I knew I needed to sit right there and soak in His peace, a peace that didn't make worldly sense. I just sat there with tears rolling down my cheeks, knowing God had transformed my life.

I was looking out of the car window at my five-bedroom house. I began to ponder, knowing just five years earlier the house before me represented a place of destruction, broken dreams and massive heartache. After seventeen years of marriage, I had discovered my family's world was crashing to an end of the life we knew. I flashed back to a past memory. I remembered that day as if it was yesterday. I had come home from work and when I walked in the door the atmosphere was so heavy, I couldn't even think or formulate a sentence. I knew something was off.

I started looking around, observing everything in the house. I noticed in the cabinet there was an empty bottle of Jack Daniels, as if it was a symbol and a declaration of the emptiness to come. I walked into the kitchen; it was a mess with mixing bowls and chocolate moulds abandoned by a guest temporarily staying in the home. My beautiful teenage daughters were still in school; their dad at work. I began to go through my normal daily routine, motions of cleaning up the house and caring for my two elderly honorary parents, an aunt and uncle, needing medical attention and medications on demand.

I can't even tell you what conversation transpired between us. I just remember walking out of their room with dirty dishes to clean and suddenly, a great spirit of heaviness fell on me and suddenly a picture of my husband with another woman flashed into my mind. I started weeping and knew the Lord was telling me, before I actually knew. 'Rebecca,' He said, 'check the phone records.' My mind raced and deep thoughts cried out, 'Please, Lord, not again!'

I went to the computer, logged in to our cell carrier, and opened the phone bill. I was shocked as I unravelled months and months of records with many women, but one in particular during the time of going to Bible study each week. It was his work desk-mate. I sobbed. I walked away from the computer and began to wander aimlessly about the house, cleaning everything in sight in a frenzy.

I took out the trash for the morning pickup in an erratic state. And then, a gust of wind came and blew open the top and little pieces of paper trash blew over the neighbourhood. It was everywhere! It seemed as if the Lord was taking me on a little prophetic walk to 'pick up the little pieces' of my heart to process with Him the reality of what was about to happen in the days ahead. My knees buckled. I found myself on the ground in the middle of the street, literally screaming at the top of my lungs. 'Why, God? How could this happen, again? Why?' I sobbed for an unknown amount of time right there, not caring if the neighbours even noticed.

I knew in my heart this was the end of my marriage. And then I found myself formulating these words aloud in a much calmer fashion, 'Lord, this hurts so much. Thank You for telling me. I know You love me. If You use this story for Your glory it will be worth it. I trust You to help me walk this out. Help me to be brave. Here I am. I am Yours and I will still praise You in this storm.'

I sat there in my car for a long moment, reminiscing over those last five years of walking out a public divorce, not just of the hardship, but in awe of how the Lord rescued us in ways no man could actually take credit for. We were scheduled to go on a family mission trip that following month. However, the girls and I went without their dad as he moved out into his new apartment. When we returned from the trip, the enemy tried to take us out, but the favour of God was so evident. He brought us through in ways that only He could, and we walked through split sea after sea. My life felt like a movie scrolling through the season.

Within days of hitting American soil, my aunt had a seizure, so we rushed to the emergency room. I heard the dreadful sound of the continuous beep from the machinery, indicating her heart stopping, and I was rushed out of the room to let the medical team in. I went out to the parking lot to pray. The phone rang and it was the girls' dad asking if I had received his email with divorce papers. It may seem random, but the enemy tried to come in like a flood, but in those times, God raises a standard (Isaiah 59:19)! The Devil's goal is to kill, steal, and destroy you (John 10:10). *But God!* Say that over your situation... *But God!* Jesus said, 'I came to give abundant life' (John 10:10).

My story didn't end here, but I have to pause for a moment and speak into your life. Let these words prophesy into your life, too. Hardship may come, but God goes before us. When we look to Him, He will rescue us and walk us through the pain to bring purpose into our lives again.

My aunt did pass away, but not that day. She came back with a strong mind and will of her own. She lived for justice and to bring the hope of Jesus Christ into the lives of others. The Lord blessed us with one more Thanksgiving together as He continued to walk me through the divorce process with a supernatural strength that could only come from Him.

In the very house that hardship came, God began to rebuild us and prepare us for a new season, full of His love and yes...His peace! My beautiful aunt and uncle purchased our home, paid for it in full, and willed it to me and left me completely debt-free. The house was gutted, emptied and no longer the same. Every light fixture had been changed and replaced. Every room was remodelled and transformed. As the house was rebuilt, so was I. I found my voice again and launched into full-time ministry.

Both daughters had gone to college with supernatural provision of full-ride scholarships. One wrote about the gift of generosity that came through our times of hardship. The other daughter was blessed as well. She was signed on the University team with a basketball scholarship and academic rewards, too. Both daughters graduated within three years of schooling with degrees and obtained great jobs. The stories behind these blessings and the people who came into our lives could only have come from the favour of the Lord.

God continued with the provision of needed cars. Not one, but through five different vehicles over the five years. At one point, I was rear-ended at a stop light. You may see this as an enemy tactic, but again, let me say, But God!' The car's value had increased due to a car shortage and after insurance I only paid $11 out of pocket for three years of using it. These were moments of miracles, and the Lord taught us to rely on Him for every step taken. Jesus supplied every need, gave us strength and so much comfort.

> Jesus said, 'Therefore everyone who hears these words of mine and puts them into practice is like a wise man who built his house on the rock. The rain came down, the streams rose, and the winds blew and beat against that house; yet it did not fall, because it had its foundation on the rock. But everyone who hears these words of mine and does not put them into practice is like a foolish man who built his house on sand. The rain came down, the streams rose, and the winds blew and beat against that house, and it fell with a great crash.'
> Matthew 7:24–27 (NIV)

As COVID came, my uncle went into hospice care, and our home became a place of ministry. While the world was shut down, the Reformation House was open. We saw so many saved, set free and delivered. Many came for hugs, fellowship and to hear the gospel. Broken bones were miraculously healed. Hearts were healed. Anyone who asked for prayer, received a touch from God. The medical providers who came didn't want to leave so lingered. People felt the tangible love of Jesus and His peace the moment they walked through the front door.

When it was my uncle's time to find his eternal home with Jesus, he was so excited that he literally passed with a smile on his face.

We mourned for him, but not nearly as much as we celebrated. His life had a great testimony and was a witness to a blessed life that blessed so many others.

> For it is by grace you have been saved, through faith
> and this is not from yourselves, it is the gift of God not
> by works, so that no one can boast.
> Ephesians 2:8–9 (NIV)

As I came back to that moment in the car, looking out at the house, I knew my life had been completely transformed. I wasn't the same person, nor did I want to be. I was happy, full of joy and filled with promises. I had learned a lot about the faithfulness of God and how great His love was for me. I learned His grace was extended to anyone who believed and truly wanted to be touched by Him. I was comfortable with who I was and had become.

I realised that not only did I feel peace but the house was a fresh representation of me. No longer a place of chaos. It was purpose-built to testify that God is good. It was there to provide others a place of rest, healing and reformation, too. It represented a fiery house of worship, gatherings and team retreats to host the glory and testimonies of Jesus. It was a place of deliverance ministry! It was a Reformation Firehouse, and I knew my story had become a testimony to many testimonies to come. God had answered my prayer. My story was for His glory.

I pray no matter what you are facing today, that you know that Jesus' love for you is greater than any circumstance. Let my testimony become your testimony. He shows no favourites (Romans 2:11). So, if He has done it for me, know here and now, He will indeed do it for you. Romans 10:13 says for 'Everyone who calls on the name of the Lord will be saved.' It says, for 'everyone'! So this means no matter who you are or where you are in life, there is redemption for you, too! God will rebuild your life and help you pick up the pieces when you turn your life back to Him.

I am so happy to report that both girls have a healthy relationship with their dad today, too. Jesus' love covers a multitude of sins and let's be honest, we all have a multitude of sins in need of undeserved forgiveness and healing. I declare the blood of Jesus over your life and situation right now and remind you again, everyone means, 'everyone'! If you don't know Him, call upon His name and let Him reveal Himself to you today. Let Him be the leader of your life. Don't look to the world for the answer, when He indeed is the answer and the God of miracles. I speak peace over every anxiety and fear, for I know He will do it for you, just as He has done it for me. Amen.

> Jesus said, 'I am leaving you with a gift, peace of mind and heart. And the peace I give is a gift the world cannot give. So don't be troubled or afraid.'
> John 14:27 (NLT)

24

The voice in the darkness

Beth's story

Waiting in the breast unit at Lincoln hospital with a friend, to see a consultant, is engraved so clearly in my memory. As I looked around – mainly at women – in the packed waiting room, I clearly remember thinking, 'There will be women in here today who are told they may have cancer; dear God, bless them, strengthen them.' The irony was, by the end of that long afternoon, I was being given a message that I never thought I would hear.

It began with a lump, a doctor's visit, then the hospital waiting room. After being examined, the consultant told me the lump was so small, his insinuation was that I was wasting their time. However, hours later, my friend had had to leave, the waiting room was now empty, and I entered a small treatment room to have a biopsy. My confidence and relief had ebbed away.

I lay on the bed while the staff chatted cheerfully, thinking of my four children, my eldest about to start secondary school, my youngest in her second year of primary. A silent tear slid down the side of my face as I tried to chat to the nurses. Within the hour, the sceptical consultant admitted they had found something worrying and I faced the realisation that the path I hoped would never be in front of me was, in fact, the one I now had to travel.

Outside, in the car park, my husband and children were waiting. As I tried to smile and we talked cheerfully about their days, I was immediately transported back to the age that my eldest daughter was now. When I was eleven, my mum had been diagnosed with breast cancer. My adolescence was filled with fear and the unknown; helpless to change anything, I grew up quickly. I finally lost my mum at 21 after a battle none of us could win. Was this going to be history repeating itself for my own children?

The results, a few days later, confirmed the consultant's view. I had breast cancer. I won't go into all the medical journey, the endless appointments, the inspirational hospital staff, the tests that seemed to show my body was hiding more than I had thought. A severe medical procedure, that was initially suggested by a stand-in consultant, had me sobbing for hours at the thought of it. Then a few short weeks later, I was begging my consultant to perform this, as my desire to survive overtook the terror.

Where was God in all of this? Right there next to me. Did I doubt His presence? No. That has never been a question for me. I first met Him and knew Him when I was six, after hearing a speaker at Birmingham Cathedral, and I still remember that moment. Since then, questioning His existence has not been my experience. I have questioned things that have happened, felt angry for the loss of my mum and wondered why things could not be different. But I have always known He was there, even in the times where I couldn't feel or hear Him directly.

So now I began a new journey. Sitting in the fear and facing the real possibility of pain and possible death. I realised, quite quickly, that although I did not feel ready to die, I could accept my own death. My real fear, the essence of which froze everything within me and caused a pain so acute in my heart that I felt that I was suffocating, was the fear of leaving my children without their mum. I had struggled so much through my teenage years, I had hardened myself and become so fiercely independent to cope with the situation. But I have felt the loss of my mum for the whole of my life, and I couldn't bear to cause that pain for my own children, as well as leaving my husband to cope with everything on his own too.

But in this situation, you have so little control, you trust in the medical expertise of those amazing professionals, but can you trust your body? Apparently not. As a healthy 41-year-old I assumed I would be fine and live a relatively long and illness-free life. The cancer card would not be dealt to me. But here I was, holding it.

Trying to explain this fear is impossible to do effectively. As a reader you may be trying to step into these words and perhaps imagine what this would look like in your situation. Or perhaps you know someone who has travelled a similar journey. However, alongside terror for me, was the guilt, guilt that my own body was negatively impacting my family. There was also loneliness, as facing possible death is something that ultimately, we must do alone.

At this exact time, the band Mumford & Sons released a new album ('Babel', 2012). One morning, I began listening to this on the way to a hospital appointment and had to pull the car over as I heard the song 'Below My Feet'. It seemed to be speaking straight from my heart.

> ...Well, I was lost,
> And now I sleep
> Sleep the hours that I can't weep
> When all I knew was steeped in blackened holes
> Well, I was lost...
> Keep the earth below my feet
> For all my sweat, my blood runs weak
> Let me learn from where I have been
> Keep my eyes to serve, my hands to learn...
> ...When I was told by Jesus, 'All was well'
> So all must be well
> Just give me time
> You know your desires and mine...
> ...For I must be well...

This summed up in every way how I was feeling. It felt, for me, as though the earth below my feet was gone, like I was falling, like there was no constant, no security, no hope, just fear and darkness. I began to sing this song regularly whenever I was alone in the car. It became a prayer, an anthem of hope. I would almost shout the line 'I must be well', I wanted that so much for my children. I could accept the ending of my life before I felt I had achieved what I wanted to, but I couldn't accept leaving my young children without a mother.

I was reminded at that time of a verse that my mum had on a card, through her illness, next to her bed. I had often read it as a teenager, and found it comforting.

> There is no one like the God of Jeshurun,
> Who rides across the heavens to help you
> And on the clouds in his majesty.
> The eternal God is your refuge,
> And underneath are the everlasting arms.
> Deuteronomy 33:26–27 (NIV)

I realised that my mum must have gone through very similar thoughts and had those same fears about leaving her children. But just as I was crying out to God for strength, I could imagine His arms below me as the ground fell away. I realised I wasn't falling, but that He was there holding me.

I would be lying if I said this suddenly made everything okay. I didn't walk around with a smile on my face, reciting Bible verses. Much of the time I felt disconnected from everything. I watched my children and pleaded for more time.

Gradually the seconds turned to minutes, the minutes to hours, then days, weeks and finally months. The medical procedures were concluded, and I was signed off from the hospital. We (and here I mean 'I') begin to take life for granted again, not as much as before, there is still a scar, but cancer fades into the background and other day-to-day features and pressures take over. So that it becomes an almost distant memory, an infrequent reminder (like when a friend asks you to write about it).

It has been nearly thirteen years since that first hospital appointment. When I think back to that time, I do immediately feel the reminder of God's presence next to me. It seems like an intensely private memory, almost difficult to articulate. That He was holding me, in the same way I would hold one of my children. That in my desperation, and I was desperate, and my vulnerability and pain, I could trust Him to be with me through it all.

All of this, has, of course, changed me. Decisions I have made since have included the self-reflection that there are no guarantees and life can become fragile or even brittle, within an instant. After this, I retrained as a psychotherapist. This added to my processing of that time and understanding how trauma can affect us, and some of the best strategies that can help us move through and make peace with thoughts and memories. I recognise that I have even greater empathy towards others, and also can see that our decisions, which might seem easy to everyone else, can be the hardest ones to make or accept. It is such a privilege to be a therapist and to be in those places with people in their darkest and most frightening times, but I can draw on God's strength as I sit in that space with them.

Many Bible verses comforted me at that time, thirteen years

ago, and have spoken to me since. I often think of Elijah in 1 Kings chapter 19. He flees for his life and in fact asks God to take it, but God sends an angel to strengthen him. He continues and eventually spends time in a cave. A windstorm passes him, but God was not in the storm. Then an earthquake, but God was not in the earthquake. Next, a mighty fire, but God was not in the fire.

Finally, he hears a gentle whisper and comes out of the cave. This is the voice of God. There are many times we can feel as though we are alone in a cave – a dark place, a lonely place. God met me in the quietness, and I heard His voice and felt His presence. That is perhaps the greatest thing that I can draw on from that time.

25

Kintsugi – mending what is broken with gold

Sandra's story

'Oh Lord, don't you dare break my heart!' I inwardly groaned as we faced my husband Chris's chance diagnosis of Chronic Myeloid Leukaemia. I saw my heart in pieces, but God's hands held all the pieces while liquid gold ran through. This was back in February 1999 – I'd never heard of kintsugi! This is our story of how faith turned painful adversity full of fragility into a space flowing with resilient peace.

So began our journey, a paradox of peace and pain!

What did that picture mean? Was Chris going to die? Was my heart about to be broken? Would it cause me to die on the inside? How would we go on? Our children were only six and four years old. In September 2000, Chris underwent a bone marrow transplant with a good non-match donor, because if he didn't, he would die within three years.

So, I'd drop the kids at school, drive an hour to Manchester to see him as he recovered and then drive back to pick up our kids at 3.30pm.

Our first pathway of peace was to keep our young children's routine as normal as possible. Over the next twenty-two months, Chris became weak with graft versus host disease due to his new immunity. He recovered some strength but in February 2002 he collapsed. As I followed the ambulance in my yellow metro, I yelled again and again, 'Oh God, please let Chris live!' He came through. Looking back, this began a new episode of graft versus host disease where his immune system attacked his lungs as though they were a threat to his health.

We'd just helped to plant Father's House, a new church born out of prophetic vision rather than division in Lancaster. Chris led worship. His heart was to open intimate times of worship to simply adore God. Chris had encouraged many young people to step into worship leading. In late May 2002, Chris had sat on a chair, playing bass in the team as he couldn't sing lead, because his breath was short. Later that day in our home, Chris spoke of how much he loved our church. This was to be the last time Chris went to church before his final journey.

The next day he was taken into hospital as doctors tried to investigate how they could help him. Our family and friends prayed, choosing to believe in healing both divine and medical. During those last two months, Rob and Anna asked me if Daddy was going to die. These were such moments of pain when I couldn't make any false promises, so I responded that I didn't know but it didn't look like that today. So as we cuddled up, we stopped to pray for Daddy's healing, full of childlike faith, the only way we knew how.

Chris was full of courage. He faced his health challenge with faith and deep assurance that God was with him. Chris was a valued employee at John Lewis, working as a computer analyst. They'd moved us north in 1997. Throughout Chris's illness the partnership fully supported us beyond expectation. It meant we could focus on trying to get Chris better. Chris expressed he was in a no-lose situation. Healing meant life and death meant eternal life. Both had pain and peace. Life with the challenges of a tampered immune system but with the joy of life together. While death meant painful separation from us but for him a release from pain into eternal peace.

This makes me remember the day we got his diagnosis. Rob was only five. Chris had just got his results, and I was in tears as I gave our lovely two their dinner. I'd turned away from the table when Rob suddenly exclaimed, 'Oh!' I assumed he'd knocked something over. This wasn't the case; instead he said, 'Mummy, God's just told me he's going to dry up all your tears.'

Like Mary, I held these words of hope in my heart. Hope of healing and life together. It wasn't until January 2003, while visiting a church in Toronto, after Chris had died at 7.27pm on the 7th day of the 7th month, did I realise that Rob had quoted a biblical verse. It says in Revelation that in heaven there's no more tears! When we listen, God speaks. He's kind and compassionate. Suddenly, I wanted to shout from the roof tops the reality of this verse, but that's another story that God was in the midst of bringing beautiful peace for us.

There were moments in Chris's last week when God's presence was so tangible, one could wonder why a loving Father didn't heal one of His children who loved Him with all of his heart, soul and strength. However, in the years since, we've chosen not to demand an answer. Some things are beyond wonder, and a definite answer is likely to bring more pain than peace.

To fall into this pit, expresses God as a divine being who at whim heals some and not others. But God is love. He perfectly created us in his image. Our bodies are intricately made, in chemical balance to live in a broken world. Yes, medicine brings hope and is an incredible gift to us, but it doesn't replace creation.

Please forgive what I'm about to say, but I remember when someone whose desire was to bring comfort, said 'God takes those he loves early sometimes.' Mama bear rose and before I could stop myself, I retorted that I didn't believe that and they were never to say that to our children. How could our God, who loved us, selfishly take Chris for himself and cause such pain to his young children. Of course, their heart was to bring comfort.

How often does desire to bring peace through misplaced compassion expose that we can't make pain better? Sometimes life is overwhelmingly painful. It just is. Pain is painful. Loss is always painful. Nothing makes it better. However, I can categorically say that God has been with us as we've chosen to lean into Him. He's held the pieces of our hearts and there's been rivers of golden love running through and overflowing. Too many stories to share in this short chapter.

As I realised that Chris was about to die, I sensed to open my Bible and read to him Revelation 4. A beautiful picture of heavenly worship. It was as though part of me touched that divine place with Chris, fully knowing God's presence. Celtic spirituality describes heaven as a paradigm just beyond our human reach as you fully stretch your arms upwards. Before I knew this I likened it to the simmering portals I'd seen on a TV sci-fi, Stargate Atlantis', as they travelled from one place to another.

Later, I would learn others describe a 'thin place'. I experienced such a thin place in those final moments. Earlier in the day, there'd been many tears as Chris and I grabbed a moment to express our love for one another. Pain and tears in his eyes as I promised to tell Rob and Anna how much their dad loved them.

Overnight, Chris had struggled to breathe, and the doctors told us his only hope was a lung transplant he couldn't have as he'd recently had a bone marrow transplant. We choked with emotion as we both sensed he was slipping away, and we made a choice not to bring our young children in to see their dad like this.

In those final moments I experienced for the first time the fullness of peace beyond all understanding. In some church traditions we pass the peace as an act of liturgy; at worst some might cringe through it or welcome an embrace to remember Christ's words. For me, I discovered the tangible peace that was beyond my capacity or ability, that has never left when I recall Chris's last breath. I know a deep assurance of joy because of the victory we have through Christ Jesus.

> And the peace of God, which transcends all understanding,
> will guard your hearts and your minds in Christ Jesus.
> Philippians 4:7 (NIV)

I know, I know, you think 'here we go again', a victorious believing Christian in denial. I'm not saying that at all. In the last twenty-three years there have been seas of tears. Just yesterday as I connected with a friend who walked through those months with us, as we remembered, tears flowed!

All those significant moments he's not been here to enjoy with me, Rob and Anna. Where was he when they needed a father's hug, affirmation or discipline? No one to bring me a cup of tea in bed. Proud moments in our kids' lives he's not been there to share. Having to be courageous at weddings, surrounded by couples having a quick hand squeeze as they remember their own vows. The moment I walked our daughter down the aisle because he couldn't, a beautiful moment laced with pain. Why did he get the easy shift while I did a double shift, having to be mum and dad?

We've muddled though. Sometimes I've made a complete mess of it; my two have chosen to forgive my lack and given me umpteen chances to have another go. Teenage emotions meant fresh pain for them. We loved being with friends, sometimes holidaying with them. Although it was normally about on day three, when I'd see the pain on their faces as they kept hearing, 'Daddy can I..., Daddy can we...,' that it would hit again: we were only three rather than four.

They've navigated life into adulthood, married their partners and now given me the joy of grandchildren. Each with their own stories of their paradox of peace and pain. They've chosen to do life filled with God's poured out love, with Jesus as their cornerstone as they build their lives on a firm foundation, knowing the storm of loss might still come close but it's not taken them out!

For me, my pathway of peace with God at my side has brought incredible joy. However, the path often intersects with another path, the pathway of pain. At these moments it's like meeting an old friend, whom with ease I journey with! My paradox of peace and pain forming in me a precious pearl of great value!

26

Finding God amongst unexpected pain and shock!

Amanda's story

Sometimes while going along in life, things happen you didn't think would, which have the power to destroy you and take you off course if you let them.

These things do not mean that God has abandoned us, sent us harm, or wants us to stay in the pain that we feel at times. It takes energy to assess, find God within the storm, and come out fighting.

I've had a desire and anticipation of being a grandmother for some time. Your children grow up, and you start to wonder what it will feel like to see and hold a newborn baby that is part of you. What will they look like? Will you have more energy? How often will you get to see them? Is the parenting going to be different from your style? Can you pass on godly influences? What a joy it will be! What a blessing!

My eldest daughter wanted to be a mother for many, many years. I also looked forward to the day when I would see her be fruitful in this role I knew she was made to be in. I had prayed into it, telling my Father how much I yearned for and wanted grandchildren, and knew it would be the making of my daughter.

Finally, in 2021, as we were driving back from Wales, she called to let us know she was pregnant. I was ecstatic and prayed virtually daily for the birth of my first grandchild. I felt I knew what his name would be. I began preparing, knitting blankets and hats, and wondering what the future would hold with a new addition to our family, thinking about the path God would lovingly create for this precious baby.

But on the day of her twelve-week scan, on my way to the supermarket, she called to say she was bleeding heavily and was waiting for an ambulance. I did not see this coming and was in total shock, 'No, Lord, this can't be happening!' She was treated poorly at the hospital. Left to sit in a corridor, bleeding through her pads and having contractions, she was told she would have to wait four hours until the time of her scheduled scan. They refused to scan her before this time.

It is a six-mile journey to the supermarket, and I was convinced if I kept praying it would turn around, but the reality started to kick in that this had actually happened, and the baby had died.

When we got to the car park, my husband asked, 'Are you coming in?' I replied 'No, I am not, I need to worship God.' I was in such grief and shock that I knew if I did not worship God right then, I didn't know if I would ever be able to again. I was crying hysterically. All worship songs went out of my head, I could not think of one. I started to panic – how could every song have left my mind so quickly?

So I just went to YouTube and typed in Psalm 23. The words were played, and I cried and cried.

When we got home, I continued in bouts of grief, my husband trying to console me but knowing there was nothing he could do practically. By bedtime, I was exhausted, and as we lay in bed looking up at the ceiling, we saw a large damp patch in our newly-decorated bedroom – a roof leak.

We had been renovating a dilapidated house for five years already, which was exhausting on top of our two full-time jobs. We had finished this room and at the time had no working bathroom, and every other room upstairs was in a complete state: no floorboards, no shower, no bath, pipes everywhere. To have this one room we could collapse in and sleep meant so much to us. So to look up to the ceiling and see that there was now an issue with the roof, which had ruined new wallpaper, and that the issue was in a complex part of the roof, I just knew this meant a lot more hard work and money at a time when I knew we had none.

It was the last straw, and I cried hysterically saying, 'God, I can't take any more!' This was at about eleven-thirty at night, and the words 'Great is thy faithfulness, O God, my Father, ... strength for today and bright hope for tomorrow' (Thomas O. Chisholm 1923) came into my spirit. They really spoke to me, and I asked Alexa to play the song on repeat. My husband, not saved yet, must have thought I was crazy but allowed me to do it. It made no sense as my first grandchild was still dead, but strength for today and bright hope for tomorrow went into my spirit. I found God. God and I connected in my dark hour, my spirit connected with His… It's what I held onto.

Every time I broke down, I kept playing it again and again, as the words are truth, and I needed that despite what had happened.

Two months later, my daughter became pregnant again. Boy, did I pray, and so did everyone I asked. I reached out to every prayer chain and group I knew, joining in their prayers. The fear that it could happen again tried to creep in, but I batted it away and refused to listen, choosing instead to trust in faith that God would not let this happen again.

However, on a Saturday, at nine-and-a-half weeks pregnant, after a private scan, she phoned to say that the baby had died in her womb. She rushed to the hospital, and again, they refused to scan her at the weekend, she had to wait until Monday. An operation to remove the tissue was then scheduled for Wednesday.

I was in shock. I had covered both babies in faith-soaked prayers, and so had all my friends. It was one of my first prayers every morning: warfaring, covering, decreeing, you name it, we bound everything!

This all took place during the depths of the COVID pandemic, when meeting others was heavily restricted. Well, you could meet, but only outside, then later inside but socially distanced. The rules kept changing. Then they weren't rules, just guidelines. I so wanted to be with my daughter, to hold her and tell her that God had a plan, but I couldn't. We had to stay away to reduce the risk of spreading the virus. I was grieving the loss of a grandchild as well as watching from afar as my daughter dealt with her extreme pain and loss. It was agony.

I went to a church meeting where people had to sit two metres apart and were not allowed to hug. I needed a hug but couldn't get one physically. People were asking, 'How is your daughter?' So kind but I was hurting so much, knowing my daughter had gone through so much pain and I could do nothing.

I sat on that chair, put my right arm out, and said, 'Father, will you hold my hand?' As I wept, I felt Him holding my hand. Two days later, I got a card in the post with this verse: 'Yet I am always with you; you hold me by my right hand. Psalm 73:23 (NIV).

Sometimes, all we can do is hold His hand and walk along with Him – no words, nothing makes sense, but He's holding my hand. I felt like I was walking through the woods with my Father in heaven, just holding hands as if I were a toddler. As I tripped up, He kept hold of my hand, and we carried on walking.

Again, no words came to explain everything, no sign that it is going to be okay. My first two grandchildren had died, my daughter was devastated, I was devastated, and didn't know why this had happened despite all the prayer covering, but my Father in heaven was holding my hand.

Sometimes the only way to see things is to know He's sovereign, and some things we cannot work out and won't get the full answer to until we stand in heaven with Him, and all things make sense.

A friend said to me, 'I see you like a strong fortress that people are looking at and turning to at this time.' I told her I didn't really feel like one some days, but I can say I have found my God through this, and I know He's holding my hand.

There was nowhere to run in the world, nothing that could give me comfort. The only thing to do is to keep worshipping Him, keep playing 'Great is thy faithfulness', keep holding His hand, and keep reading His word. And to keep giving Him my tears until one day they will slow down and stop.

Two months after the second miscarriage, she became pregnant again. The hospital had carried out testing after the second miscarriage and found a chromosomal abnormality. This time she was closely monitored, and extra support was in place from the perinatal services. My beloved grandson was born on my birthday – how special is that!

It tested my faith, to start believing again, to believe that yes, all my prayers and the prayers of others would make a difference. I would not live in fear that this would happen again, but I could fully throw myself on my God and Father and fully trust Him.

When we go through things, finding God, feeling God, sensing God, can sometimes be all we have to hold onto, but it's enough to get you through. It doesn't stop the pain, but the word says: 'They triumphed over him by the blood of the Lamb and by the word of their testimony.' Revelation 12:11 (NIV).

Expanding our family has brought us all closer together. We've been blessed by the joy my grandson brings, and our family now meets once a month and video calls far more often. We have amazing plans for the future and have begun creating new family traditions. Bringing him into church when they visit has filled me with such delight and wonder, seeing the answer to our prayers reflected in him and sharing that joy with friends and others at church. I am so proud of my daughter and how she coped.

I hope my story encourages you to be able to know that God is sovereign, and we don't understand everything, that's all.

> Yours, LORD, is the greatness and the power and the glory and the majesty and the splendour, for all in heaven and earth is Yours. Yours, LORD is the kingdom; You are exalted as head over all.
> 1 Chronicles 29:11 (NIV)

God is still there for you and sees every tear you cry:

> You keep track of all my sorrows; you have collected all my tears in your bottle. You have recorded each one in your book.'
> Psalm 56:8 (NLT).

The question is, will we continually be with Him? In His presence, in His word? Will we run to Him in times of shock and turmoil? Will we accept His sovereignty?

Holding onto God's hand during hardship, immersing ourselves in His words of wisdom and love, we can trust that no matter the journey, He has a plan for us. Even in our darkest hour, the Lord is by our side, holding a guiding flame to light the way.

27

Unanswered questions

Foulkes's story

Can we read God's mind? Sometimes it's difficult to know if it's God speaking or not!

My faith journey has been asking if God intervenes, or is cause and effect the law we have to live with? Is there even a black-and-white answer to this?

God has created us to live by the rules of creation. Sometimes God does intervene sovereignly. If God always intervened, there would be an unbridgeable gap between free will and determinism.

When I was younger, I believed in more binary and clear lines of how God works. When I did something, it was either right or wrong, wise or unwise. God was always assessing me or sometimes judging me. Have we lived with this in the West for years? Our default position is to plead for God's mercy as sinners. Rather, I believe that the nature of love in 1 Corinthians 13 starts and ends with grace rather than condemnation. Sin should not be neglected, but it comes to the surface as we trust God's loving nature fully.

Our early marriage was difficult because of me. My doubts and past kept taking centre stage. After we'd been married for three or four months, I began to think that I'd made a terrible mistake. 'Where was God now?' I kept asking.

I was in serious difficulty and, of course, it was tough for my wife too. I went for counselling and advice from a wise man, who was not in the least bit fazed by what I said. I even told him about my wild days as a teenager, getting myself into serious unintended liaisons that weren't good.

We prayed together and I prayed that I would properly fall in love with my wife so that I could then leave behind previous connections and behaviour. It was a long journey. Perhaps time and distance also healed, but I realised it was about changing me from within and being prepared to make an adjustment, rather than looking for some excuse. So, did God answer my prayer? Was it from the hard work I did or was it God or both? Since that time, I have had a deep love for my wife which has never been compromised.

It was about changing me, a process that was gradual, no shaft of bright light. It took time and needed an awareness that I was in trouble and I needed to get it sorted. God was gracious. The help of a friend, hard work and prayer brought me through to a place of breakthrough into a beautiful relationship.

Many years later, and about two months into starting a new business that wasn't going well, we were losing money weekly. We had a manager who was only just coping, lacking some essential skills. Suddenly he rang up, saying he was unwell and that he couldn't work for us anymore. This seemed devastating and we received prayer from friends, yet it did force us to take a fresh look at the business. You could say God caused the manager to resign, but I don't believe that. His health was bad, and his commute wasn't sustainable. Yet God used this to reorientate us and our business.

Looking back, I can see the hand of God through cause and effect. This then led to a healthy business. We were trusting God, but I don't think I would now ask the question of whether it was God, as now I just take what He gives. How do we learn and grow in our faith? My faith was immature at the time. The teaching I'd had had been lacking in the mystery of God. I needed to be able to live without having to answer all the questions. Living with wonder, uncertainty is fundamental.

Years later, my faith matured during the pain of a church split I was quite closely involved in. When I got to the point that I stopped seeking justice and blaming others, I took a look inside myself and what I found was big. I realised I'd held others in judgement, both overtly and subconsciously.

What I thought had been a raft of good relationships, suddenly ceased to exist. I became a pariah. Yes, I'd been unwise, not consciously, but I can now see there were cracks in the system and I didn't react as I should have done. I was seen as a threat or an enemy, at least that was my perception. We were no longer wanted and were left alone. We were no longer in the inner ring; we were out. But it wasn't all bad. God still blessed others during this time of split – isn't that amazing? Never underestimate God's ability to bless, even when the channels of blessing are flawed people – as we all are!

In a way, this is the time I most encountered God – when I was willing to take an inner journey and address some of the shadows in my life and personality. I must add that counselling also helped me on my healing and maturing journey. With honesty and openness to one's own shadow self, I met grace rather than condemnation. That was God revealing himself in the things that needed to change. We are all in the business of transformation, aren't we?

God didn't seem interested in my sense of justice. Actually, he told me He loved me, unconditionally. Whatever I'd done or thought, I was called to move on. I did realise I had to look at myself and my part in the situation. God was both forgiving and whatever part I'd played, it wasn't my business. I was in a close and abiding relationship with Him, and this wasn't affected by what had happened. Any mistakes or wrong attitudes don't affect God's ability to meet you with grace.

As a result, I became distinctly uncomfortable in churches. This is one reason my wife and I went to plant a church. Getting away was such a help, being away from the labels and stereotypes. A curate said to my wife one Sunday, 'Oh... I've heard of you, your reputation follows you.' It was distinctly uncomfortable.

After four years of completing the plant, trying to integrate in a church was such a challenge. It took years for us to find a church where we felt accepted.

Where was God in this journey? He wants the church, His body, to be as healthy as possible, but sometimes, His children live quite lonely lives. I have met many wonderful Christians over the years who haven't fitted into the church locally. It's not a problem for me. Is it a problem to God? I don't think so. Life, again, is a mystery.

I had a deep sense of God's presence and peace whether I was in church or not. It was like a carefree sense of joy, expressible through difficult times.

I can work with sadness, but I carry a deep and abiding joy. Life is sad at times, many times. We all have our shadows, thought lives, difficulties. This doesn't impede God's grace and blessing. Paul was hard pressed yet content, wasn't he? The things he worked and strove for were his sense of calling and he was given strength for every day: 'I have learned the secret of being content in any and every situation.' Philippians 4:12 (NIV)

Are we looking for perfectionist Christianity? Do we feel that if we don't feel worthy, we are second best or at the bottom of the pile? That isn't what Jesus says – I come for the lost, the least of the brethren.

28

Finding me: a tale of broken bones, broken past and boundless grace

Rowena's story

In 2022, I was sitting watching TV and I suddenly realised I couldn't lift my arms. They were tingly yet unresponsive to my nonverbal demand. I remember screaming internally at my arms to touch my head. No response.

This was a new and frightening symptom for me. I'd been working in education for many years, and as a deputy headteacher of a large primary school, working over seventy hours a week, I wasn't coping with the workload, or with life!

I was undergoing investigation following an episode of burnout, with so many physical symptoms, including loss of vision in one eye, chest pain that was very strong and frightening, and pounding headaches. I felt such shame at not being able to cope. I was letting my team down. I was so weak and I was a failure. I felt guilty for not working. Where was my identity now? I felt fear: what if I didn't get better? Was I still likeable? Lovable? So many people, both work colleagues and those closer to me, had deserted me at that point. It seemed they didn't like this version of me. Could I blame them? I didn't like this version of me either!

I felt overwhelmed by grief and loss at leaving a job I loved. My old inner critic came back so strongly – I'm not good enough, I've let people down. I was trapped in physical pain and restriction.

Where was God? Yet God was the one who I could cry out to about how desperate I really felt. Through the sleepless nights, and when I felt so isolated. With him I didn't need to pretend that I was OK or even coping... I wasn't!

I started to journal more regularly. I wrote down daily how I was, and I started noticing, as I looked back, that I was indeed moving forward, even if I didn't feel like it on that particular day. I didn't see a miracle in the classic sense of healing in that moment. Yet I've had my own miracle. That is evident looking back over that time.

I believe the devil tried to bring me down, but just as Joseph says: 'You intended to harm me, but God intended it for good.' Genesis 50:20 (NIV). God had another plan.

Over many months, with more loss and rejection and self-doubt, I've emerged with a clearer insight into what it means for me to be a child of God, the daughter of the King, the beloved of the Almighty. My identity is in who Christ says I am, not who my inner critic says, and also not what other people might think or at times tell me I am.

I am loved, I am strong, I am held, I belong to the King of Kings.

But my journey didn't stop there. We are constantly learning, growing and being transformed into the likeness of Jesus, aren't we?

More recently, I had an extraordinary insight into the goodness of God. I'd lived for years with an increasingly painful hand and wrist that was making many things difficult – like driving, swimming and eating. Getting dressed needed a deep breath and sometimes I'd sleep in my clothes, so I didn't have to face the pain of undressing. The surgeons found, after an initial failed surgery, that I had a rare condition and they planned to re-operate. This came at a time when I was dealing with a second divorce, having to sell the house we'd bought together and trying to find a new, safe place to live, and simply to try to rebuild my life.

Where is God when your life comes crashing down, hopes are dashed, and joy seems to have left the building? The reality of divorce is that some friends can't handle it/you/the fall-out and others step into the gaps.

The Bible says that 'weeping may stay for the night, but rejoicing comes in the morning.' Psalm 30:5 (NIV). The Message version of this verse says, 'The nights of crying your eyes out give way to days of laughter.'

How can we manage through the night until the morning, especially when the morning seems to be taking a very long time?

Life is a roller-coaster sometimes, isn't it? Friends stepped in to plug the gaps. My church family simply turned up to pack up my house and move me into my new one. My kids were brilliant, turning up to take me to surgeries, tag-teaming to support me and checking up on their old mama daily.

I also had a counsellor who held me and guided me through this time. Planning small steps was empowering, taking responsibility for my own thoughts and actions, and learning to hand the pain to God daily.

Is it morning yet? It there joy yet? Psalm 30:4 (NIV) says, 'Sing praises of the Lord, you his faithful people; praise his holy name.' This comes just before we are told that joy comes in the morning. How do we, might we, or can we praise God when it still feels like nighttime?

I have learnt to praise God for who He is, for the people He has put in my life, for the small things. I remember one day post-surgery, a friend popped in with a meal, opened a bottle of fizzy water, filled my coffee machine and changed my bedding. These were all things I was unable to do myself, and I felt so loved. Was this the joy spoken of in Psalm 30? She was Jesus' hands and feet to me.

After that surgery to remove a bone from my hand that had basically died (the non-medical term!), the surgeon explained to me that he had to pick out all the dead fragments of bone and then he covered it and the surrounding area with metal to strengthen it. The result for me was both disappearance of pain and a hand that I can now use. Amazing, right?!

As I sat around waiting for my wrist to heal post-surgery, I realised that this is a symbol of what Jesus has done for me – for each of us! When Jesus left the grave behind and came back to life, after spending three days in Hell, He ensured all my past mistakes, my shame and my disappointments were left behind. I don't get to choose which I keep and which I let go, He took them all. His blood covers our scars.

As I came to accept fully the completeness of the forgiveness that I am offered (part of this is to learn to forgive myself, which I found harder), I have become more aware both of the fact that it's ok to be vulnerable and that as I become stronger I can learn to be a better version of me.

My journey has been one of thinking or believing that I am a second-class citizen because of my past. My success is my four wonderful grown children. Yet I also have two divorces and two episodes of burnout where I badly let down my colleagues in school.

I have always tried to fit in, to mould myself to be who everyone else wanted me to be. Life is easier that way! It means I can generally avoid confrontation, but this does mean I have found myself doing things that don't sit well with me.

Don't get me wrong, I praised and prayed my way into school every day for many years as a teacher and finally as a deputy headteacher. I absolutely loved what I did, it was my passion. I spent my days looking after the children, their families and of course the staff. What I forgot was that I also have value and needed looking after. Subconsciously, I sought value from unhealthy places – for me this wasn't money or success, but instead saying yes to everything I was asked to do, working extremely long hours, trying to be the solution to everybody's problems.

The amazing news is that once we accept the fullness of the message of the Cross, that we are totally forgiven, that Jesus dies for every single one of us, just as we are, then we can become the best version of ourselves. This means that rather than trying to be a version of me that suits others, I submit to God and stand on His promises. For me, this means that I do not live in fear of or in submission to others and their expectations or opinions. Rather, I let go of my inner critic and I have had to say sorry to God for not having allowed Him into every area of my life, including the shame, guilt and failures. Moving on from this, I open up possibilities of a new outlook and a less messy thought life.

Having fought insignificance my whole life, I now wake up daily accepting that I have been given qualities, even those of a Proverbs 31 woman. I still have doubts and fears, but I speak over them words such as 'I am a beloved of Christ'. That's what the Bible says!

Song of Songs 8:5 reads, 'Who is this coming up from the wilderness leaning on her beloved?' I have realised that as I lean on Jesus, I become unrecognisable to those who knew me in the past. The more I lean, the more I am transformed into His likeness. In reality, this is messy of course. Daily I journal. As I look back, I see words such as exhausted, inadequate, tears, loss, shame, disappointment and rejection.

However, more recently I have recognised that God has dealt with my past and it is time to let go. I remember my value is based on an empty grave, a promise that I am a new creation. I am completely forgiven (not partially) and my value comes from being His child and

His beloved. So, words more recently have been: building, new, pivot, joy, preparation, and I have started to dream again. Daily, as my mind is restored and healed, I can accept that I have the mind of Christ and this opens up immense opportunities for me.

In Luke 22:32 (NIV) Jesus said, 'I have prayed for you, Simon, that your faith may not fail.' Jesus knew that Simon Peter was about to fail and yet Jesus still picked him. Peter's success depended on Jesus' faith rather than Peter's. Peter must have felt such a failure after he disowned Jesus three times, and I have lived as if I was a failure for so long. However, Jesus says our success is to demonstrate God's glory which I can't fully do if I haven't given God all my anxiety, my failures or my shame.

Am I sorted? I am a work in progress. My confidence comes from knowing I am valued by God. I may not always be accepted on earth, but Jesus wasn't either, was He? Galatians 5 says that 'It is for freedom that Christ has set us free.' (NIV)

I am challenged therefore to live as a free child of God. I had been putting myself on trial daily, asking myself if I was good enough in the world's eyes. Too often I used to come up with a *no* in answer to my trial. Not any more!

Jesus looks at you and me, not looking at our performance, and only *His* opinion counts. He says we are enough, just as we are. Jesus has faith in me and you – what a revelation!

Before I finish, can I speak specifically to some of those reading this? Are you divorced or do you know someone who is? After my first divorce I encountered much condemnation and criticism, mostly from Christians. You don't need to tell me that this isn't God's perfect plan, yet it happens. My precious Aunt Anne suggested I attend a Restored Lives group for those going through divorce and separation. I could hardly walk into the hall as I felt such shame, guilt and regret. All I can remember from that night was a young man standing up and telling us that through his story of loss and pain, Jesus still loved him. That evening, I realised that even when we mess up hugely, Jesus doesn't give up on us. He still loved me!

If Jesus went to the grave for our failures, mistakes and shame, we must agree today not to sit in that grave space, but to stand up bravely, just as Peter did in Acts 2. Understanding our own value is seeing and understanding that we don't have to do life in our own strength. I don't have to work harder to strive to please or prove my worth to others. God loves me already and I am made to glorify God.

Success is opening the lid of the grave, letting Jesus take us by the hand, for Him to pull or lift us out of that space from where He says, 'strengthen your brothers'. (Luke 22:32, NIV).

St. Irenaeus, Bishop of Lyon said, 'The glory of God is man fully alive'. As we live fully and in alignment with God's will, we truly honour Him.

Next steps...

Dear Friend,

If you've read this book and realised you don't yet have a personal relationship with God, but you'd like to, this is a beautiful moment to take that step. God loves you deeply and is waiting to walk with you on this new journey.

You can begin by simply talking to Him, ask Him to come into your life and forgive you. Here's a short prayer you can use to help you (say it from your heart):

Dear Father God,

Thank You for loving me. I want to know You and experience Your love in my heart. Please forgive me for my sins. Thank You for sending Your Son, Jesus, to die on the cross for my sins and to give me new life. Today, I open my heart and invite Jesus to be my Lord and Saviour. Thank You for giving me hope, a fresh start, and eternal life. Please guide me and help me become the person You created me to be. Amen.

If you prayed the above prayer, congratulations and welcome to God's family! Here are a few simple ways to help you grow in your new relationship with Him:

Talk to God every day: Prayer is just having an honest conversation with God. Share your thoughts, worries, and joys with Him, He loves to listen. Remember, Christianity is about relationship, not rules. As you talk to God, you'll start to sense His peace and encouragement in your heart.

Read the Bible to get to know Him better: the Bible is God's Word, your guidebook for life. Start by reading a little each day. The Gospels (Matthew, Mark, Luke, and John) are a great place to begin. You'll learn about Jesus and how much He cares for you.

Here are a few verses to encourage you in your faith journey: John 3:16; John 17:3; Romans 3:23; Romans 6:23; Romans 10:9–10; 2 Corinthians 5:17–21; and Ephesians 2:8–9.

Find a community of believers: Look for a local church that teaches from the Bible. Being around other Christians will encourage you and help your faith grow.

Here's to your new life in Christ, full of hope, love and purpose!

Printed in Dunstable, United Kingdom

71094711R00087